PRAYING TO OUR LORD JESUS CHRIST

FR. BENEDICT J. GROESCHEL, C.F.R.

PRAYING
TO
OUR LORD
JESUS CHRIST

Prayers and Meditations through the Centuries

IGNATIUS PRESS   SAN FRANCISCO

Cover art:
Detail of Christ from the *Deesis*
(Christ, Mary, and John the Baptist),
from the north gallery.
Byzantine mosaic, 12th century.
Hagia Sophia / Istanbul, Turkey
© Erich Lessing / Art Resource, New York

Cover design by Roxanne Mei Lum

To Jesus of Nazareth,
our Brother,
our Messiah,
our Savior,
our Redeemer,
our Eternal King

CONTENTS

A WORD OF THANKS

This book was written under rather difficult circumstances. I had been hospitalized for some months as a result of a severe automobile accident in January 2004. I did, however, want to bring out a small book of prayers to Christ in order to encourage every Catholic, every Christian, to pray devoutly and fervently every day to Christ as our brother, our Savior, our Redeemer, and our divine Lord and Master. *The Passion of the Christ*, a recent film, had a profound effect on many people and reminded all of us of what Christ did in giving His life for us. It preached loudly the words of Scripture, "For God so loved the world that he gave his only Son" (Jn 3:16).

I wish to thank all who have helped me with this book: my staff and colleagues at Trinity Retreat and James Monti, who provided valuable research. I am also deeply grateful to Ignatius Press for seeing the book to publication so quickly, thereby facilitating its wide circulation among the faithful.

Let us pray to Christ every day, let us pray for each other and for the world. He, the Son of God, stands at the center of the world in the mystery of His birth, His holy life, His terrible death, and His glorious Resurrection and Ascension. These are the beginning mysteries of the Paschal Mystery, in which you and I hope to participate for all eternity.

Praised be Jesus Christ, now and forever! Amen.

INTRODUCTION

If we believe that Jesus Christ is the Son of God, our Lord and Savior who has called us back from eternal death and given us the promise of eternal life, and if we believe that He died for our sins on the Cross, then nothing is more obvious than that we should pray to Him. Prayers to Jesus have been characteristic of Christian people since the earliest days. This little prayer book is meant for those who would like to pray to Jesus and to develop their own prayer to Him, which in some ways is the most effective.

The Christian is a devoted person—devoted to God, to our Lord Jesus Christ, to the Blessed Virgin Mary, and to the angels and saints. Our devotion grows as we increase in our realization that our God is a personal God, whose love for us is infinite. He has "wondrously created us and even more wondrously redeemed us", as Saint Leo put it. He has taken great care in our creation and, in the divine Person of Christ, has suffered great pain in our redemption. Christ is the incarnate revelation of the Father's love for us. It is impossible that our God could be indifferent to us at any stage of our existence. We are "enfolded in his love", as Julian of Norwich said, and our heavenly Father rewards even the smallest of good deeds done in secret (Mt 6:3).

The essential element of devotion is trust, and our Lord bids us, in the Sermon on the Mount, to have trust above all in our heavenly Father, whose loving Providence extends even to the birds of the air and the lilies of the field. "Are you not of more value than they?" He asks (Mt 6:26).

Cardinal Newman has a fitting description of devotion

that is helpful to call often to mind, illustrating both the importance of devotion in our Christian life and the spring from which it flows.

> God beholds thee individually, whoever thou art. He "calls thee by thy name". He sees thee, and understands thee, as He made thee. He knows what is in thee, all thy own peculiar feelings and thoughts, thy dispositions and likings, thy strength and thy weakness. He views thee in thy day of rejoicing, and thy day of sorrow. He sympathizes in thy hopes and thy temptations. He interests Himself in all thy anxieties and remembrances, all the risings and fallings of thy spirit. He has numbered the very hairs of thy head and the cubits of thy stature. He compasses thee round and bears thee in His arms; He takes thee up and sets thee down. He notes thy very countenance, whether smiling or in tears, whether healthful or sickly. He looks tenderly upon thy hands and thy feet; He hears thy voice, the beating of thy heart, and thy very breathing. Thou dost not love thyself better than He loves thee. Thou canst not shrink from pain more than He dislikes thy bearing it; and if He puts it on thee, it is as thou wilt put it on thyself, if thou art wise, for a greater good afterwards.[1]

Prayer is the lifting of the heart and mind to God; therefore, it is also the lifting of the heart and mind to Jesus Christ, as He is now in eternal glory. We can pray to Him as we recall the past events of His life. When the film *The Passion of the Christ*

[1] John Henry Newman, "A Particular Providence as Revealed in the Gospel", *Parochial and Plain Sermons* (San Francisco: Ignatius Press, 1997), 562–63.

was being shown, friends of mine attended a late evening performance. Seated next to them were some young African American fellows dressed in the colorful way of teenagers today. All during the film they spoke out loud to Jesus; it was very impressive. "You tell them, Jesus"; "O Jesus, don't let them do that to you." They knew how to speak to Jesus Christ, even though, from their appearance, they did not seem to be particularly religious young men. They had learned this way of speaking at home and in their humble Gospel church. It was very moving to the people around them.

At this time in the Church it seems to me that we need to bring back devotion, especially devotion to Jesus Christ. I have written a larger book, which will be published soon, on the history of Catholic, Protestant, and Orthodox devotion to Jesus Christ. I had intended to publish this present book of prayers after that book was finished, but because of recent injuries I decided to do this book first and make it available before the larger book comes out.

The First Prayer to Jesus

The first prayer recorded in Sacred Scripture that is addressed to Jesus Christ ascended to the heavenly Father is said by Saint Stephen, a young man about to be stoned for his loyalty to Christ. An analysis of that event proves helpful, because Stephen is aware of Christ's presence. He sees Him standing in the heavens. Stephen is doing what Christ has asked him to do, namely, forgiving his enemies, which to the people of the time must have seemed like an odd demand. Finally, as he is dying, he trusts himself completely to Jesus. This is a powerful example of true Christian devotion. The text, which is repeated here, is worth looking at in the light of what we are saying.

But he, full of the Holy Spirit, gazed into heaven and saw the glory of God, and Jesus standing at the right hand of God; and he said, "Behold, I see the heavens opened, and the Son of man standing at the right hand of God." But they cried out with a loud voice and stopped their ears and rushed together upon him. Then they cast him out of the city and stoned him; and the witnesses laid down their garments at the feet of a young man named Saul. And as they were stoning Stephen, he prayed, "Lord Jesus, receive my spirit." And he knelt down and cried with a loud voice, "Lord, do not hold this sin against them." And when he had said this, he fell asleep (Acts 7:55–60).

Anyone who wishes to pray to Jesus and grow closer through prayer to our Lord and Savior will find the prayers in this book helpful. They are culled from various periods in the twenty-one centuries of Christianity.

How to Use This Book

This book contains the prayers of other people, some of them monks, some of them theologians, some of them saints. The prayers are intended for meditation, and the book would probably be most helpful to people if it is used with that purpose in mind. In that way you would be doing more than simply saying prayers—you would be making the prayers your own. It isn't always helpful to read prayers written by other people, although it is certainly a way of devotion. Eventually, we have to make other people's words our own, or our prayer will become extremely dry. How rewarding it is to meditate on beautiful prayers so that our own prayers may become more meaningful.

We have included prayers from different ages of the Church, from people in very different circumstances, all of whom were united in the fact that they believed in Jesus as the Son of God and wanted to know Him better. How important it is then for us to try to grow with Jesus and increase our knowledge of Him. This book is meant to help you do exactly that. It is also meant to deepen your prayer life. You may not have thought of using some of the prayers given here; some of the ways of praying may not have seemed very realistic to you. These prayers will help you understand how Christians throughout the ages have lifted their hearts and minds to Jesus Christ.

At the conclusion of the book are quotations from the Church's treasury of dogmatic and doctrinal teachings, as well as from more contemporary writings, especially from those of Pope John Paul II. A profound devotion marks the Holy Father's writings and has been, thankfully, a counterweight to theological theories and scriptural speculations that have tended to undermine belief in devotion to Jesus Christ.

A CHRISTIAN MARTYR | *Ernst Slingeneyer (1820–1894)*

THE EARLY MARTYRS

Among the earliest prayers we have to Jesus Christ are those recorded of the martyrs. Obviously, we cannot be sure that they were recorded or have come down to us exactly as they were given. In the various martyrologies and accounts of the martyrs, there seems to be a common theme, which we have seen in Saint Stephen: the martyrs are aware of Christ's presence, they obey Him, and they trust their souls to Him, because they are going to perish in this world.

I think this theme makes up the essential devotion to Jesus Christ. We must remember that there were also many martyrs in the twentieth century, some of whom were killed, others imprisoned for many years. All offered their lives to Christ in obedience to the requirements of faith.

Steep yourself in the sense of the martyrs. You will find that your faith will grow, and the trials of life will not seem so heavy.

Lord God Almighty, Father of Jesus Christ, that dear Child of yours, through whom we have come to know you, God of the angels and powers, God of all creation, God of the race that lives in your presence, the race of the just.

I bless you because you have thought me worthy . . . to be numbered among the martyrs and to drink out of the cup your Anointed has drunk from. . . . For this and all your blessings I praise you and give you glory, through the eternal high priest, Jesus Christ the heavenly, your dear Child.

He is with you and the Holy Spirit. Through him may glory be given you now and in the ages to come. Amen.[1]

Saint Polycarp
Bishop of Smyrna, one of the Apostolic Fathers (d. *c.* 155)

Christ became man by the Virgin so that the disobe- dience which proceeded from the serpent might be destroyed in the same way as it originated. For Eve, being a virgin and undefiled, having conceived the word from the serpent, brought forth disobedience and death. The Virgin Mary, however, having received faith and joy, when the angel Gabriel announced to her the good tidings . . . answered: "Be it done unto me according to thy word." [2]

Saint Justin
Apologist and martyr (second century)

How happy Christ was to be there, how gladly he fought and conquered in such servants! He protects their faith and gives strength to believers in proportion to the trust that each man who receives that strength is willing to place in him. Christ was there to wage his own battle; he aroused the soldiers who fought for his name; he made them spirited and strong. And he who once for all has conquered death for us, now continually conquers in us.[3]

King of the saints,
invisible Word of the Father most High,
wisdom's Prince, Ground of exertion, eternal Joy;
Jesus, Saviour of this mortal race,
you the Shepherd, Cultivator,
you the Helmsman and the Rider,
you the Wing that lifts to heaven
all the company of the saints;
Fisher of men;
them you came to deliver from the waters of sin;
to fish untainted by the envious sea
you cast the bait of sweet fresh life.
Guide your flock of spiritual sheep;
guide, holy King, guide your unsullied children.
The prints of Christ's feet show the way to heaven.
Word everlasting, Age without end, undying Light,
Fountain of mercy, Doer of virtuous deeds,
exalted Life of them that sing God's praises. . . .
Let us together sing simple praises,
true hymns to Christ the King. . . .[4]

Saint Cyprian
Bishop of Carthage (d. 258)

L ord Jesus Christ, who hast made heaven and earth, and who never forsakest those who hope in thee, I give thee thanks that thou hast granted me to conquer the dragon and to crush his head. Give rest to thy servants, grant that I may be the last victim of the violence of our enemies. Give peace to thy Church, snatch her from the tyranny of the devil. Amen.[5]

Theodotus of Ancyra
Martyr, tavern keeper (d. *c.* 302)

O Lord God Almighty, Jesus Christ, who didst come to call not the just but sinners to repentance, thus confirming the promise thou didst vouchsafe to make saying, "In the hour when the sinner shall repent of his sins, in that same hour I will no more remember them," accept at this hour my martyrdom as a penance, and by the material fire prepared for my body deliver me from the everlasting fire which burns both body and soul.

I give thee thanks, Lord Jesus Christ, that thou hast vouchsafed to accept me as a victim for the glory of thy name, thou who wast offered as Victim on the cross for the salvation of the whole world, the Just for the unjust, the Good for the wicked, the Blessed One for the cursed, the Innocent for the guilty. I offer my sacrifice to thee, who with the Father and the Holy Ghost livest and reignest God for ever and ever. Amen.[6]

Saint Afra
Martyr, Augsburg, Germany (d. early fourth century)

INTRODUCTION TO THE FATHERS

Included in the Church Fathers are a large number of people who were martyrs. There is a difference between them and the early martyrs, however: the Church Fathers began early to contribute to the theology of Christianity and the interpretation of the Gospels and the New Testament, which had yet to be codified. We see this in the prayers of Saint Ignatius of Antioch and other early Fathers, who gave up their lives and used their talents, under the inspiration of the Holy Spirit, to add to the richness of Christian life in the early centuries. Their prayers had a profound effect because they indicated the direction that prayer to Christ would take in the future.

As the Church came out of the persecutions, it quickly became theologically richer. An incredible group of men began writing for the Church, and many of them became bishops and popes. These are usually referred to as the Fathers of the Church. They range from Saint John Chrysostom, bishop and patriarch of Constantinople, to Saint Augustine, bishop of Hippo. They were often gifted young converts from paganism or from a worldly life, and their prayers are most revealing and directly related to what they thought about life.

Although we are reading these prayers some sixteen hundred years after they were written, they frequently refer to experiences and emotions that are familiar to us. The immense treasure left by the Fathers has guided and fed the Church for many centuries. Unfortunately, people are not aware enough of their writings.

If you are moved by the prayers of the Church Fathers, I suggest you go to a Catholic bookstore and buy some of their writings.

2

THE FATHERS OF THE EAST

And so he was raised on a cross, and a title was fixed, indicating who it was who was being executed. Painful it is to say, but more terrible not to say. . . . He who suspended the earth is suspended; he who fixed the heavens is fixed; he who fastened all things is fastened to the wood; the Master is outraged; God is murdered.[1]

Melito of Sardis
Bishop in Asia Minor (second century)

We do not worship a creature. Far be the thought! For such an error belongs to heathens and Arians. But we worship the Lord of Creation, Incarnate, the Word of God. For if the flesh also is in itself a part of the created world, yet it has become God's body. And we neither divide the body, being such, from the Word, and worship it by itself, nor when we wish to worship the Word do we set Him far apart from the Flesh, but knowing . . . that "the Word was made flesh" (Jn 1:14) we recognise Him as God also, after having come in the flesh.[2]

Saint Athanasius
Bishop of Alexandria (b. *c.* 295, d. 373)

THE GOOD SAMARITAN | *Early 6th century*

Lord Christ our God, King of the ages and Creator of all, I thank You for the blessings You have granted me and for the communion of Your pure and life-giving Mysteries. I pray You, therefore, gracious Lord and Lover of mankind, guard me under Your protection and within the shadow of Your wings; and grant me with a clear conscience till my last breath worthily to partake of Your sacred Gifts for forgiveness of sins and for life eternal. For You are the Bread of Life, the Source of Holiness, the Giver of all that is good, and to You we send up the glory, with the Father and the Holy Spirit, now and ever and to the ages of ages. Amen.[3]

Saint Basil the Great
Bishop of Caesarea (b. *c.* 329, d. 379)

O Lord Jesus Christ . . .
be merciful and forgive me, Your unworthy servant,
if somehow I have sinned this day as a human,
or rather as an inhuman.
Forgive my voluntary and involuntary sins,
the ones I have committed in knowledge or in ignorance,
the ones that have been done
out of evil influences and carelessness
and my great indolence and negligence.
Forgive me, O Lord,
if I have taken an oath by Your holy name
or if I have violated my oath;
if I have sworn in my mind
or if I have somehow irritated You;
if I have stolen
or if I have lied;
if a friend came to me and I ignored him
or if I have distressed and embittered my brother; . . .
if I looked upon vain beauty
and my mind was attracted by it;
if I was overly talkative about improper things
or if I busied myself with the faults of my brother
and condemned him
while overlooking my own innumerable faults;
if I have neglected my prayer
or if I have brought to mind any other evil thing.
Forgive me, O God,
your useless servant,
all these and whatever other things
I have done and do not remember.
Have mercy on me, O Lord,
for You are good and You love mankind,
so that I, the prodigal one,

may go to bed and fall asleep
glorifying You,
together with the Father
and Your all-holy, good and life-creating Spirit,
now and ever and unto the ages of ages. Amen.[4]

I give you glory, O Christ, because you, the Only Begotten, the Lord of all things, who alone are without sin, gave yourself to die for me, a sinner, unworthy of such a blessing: you died the death of the cross to free my sinful soul from the bonds of sin.

What shall I give you, Lord, in return for all this kindness?
Glory to you for your love.
Glory to you for your mercy.
Glory to you for your patience.
Glory to you for forgiving us all our sins.
Glory to you for coming to save our souls.
Glory to you for your incarnation in the virgin's womb.
Glory to you for your bonds.
Glory to you for receiving the cut of the lash.
Glory to you for accepting mockery.
Glory to you for your crucifixion.
Glory to you for your burial.
Glory to you for your resurrection.
Glory to you that were preached to men.
Glory to you in whom they believed.
Glory to you that were taken up into heaven.[5]

Saint Ephrem the Syrian
(306–373)

O Christ my King. You turned aside the dire might of Amelech, when your servant Moses raised his pure hands after the pattern of the cross in prayer upon the mountain. You fettered the savage jaws of lions and the sharp strength of their claws for Daniel's sake when he stretched out his hands. When Jonas opened wide his arms in prayer within the monster's entrails, he was delivered by your power from the whale. . . . Once, in order to deliver the storm-tossed disciples from the waters, you trod on foot the face of the turbulent deep stilling the waves' and the winds' might. For many a person you have rescued soul and body from disease. You who are God became man and mingled with mortals.

God from all time, you were manifested to us in the fulness of time. . . . Thus, when I call on you, come as blessed and propitious God. Come to me with helping hand, O my propitious God. Save me, overwhelmed as I am amid war, and wild beasts, and fire, and storm. I have nowhere to turn my gaze except to God alone. All this is brought upon me by evil men, the destroyers of life. . . . Their chief animosity is directed against people who love God. . . .

From these, O Christ, deliver me. Spread your sheltering wings about me always. O King, drive hateful cares far from your servant. Let not my mind be harassed by grave anxieties, such as this world and the prince of this world devise for hapless mortals.[6]

Saint Gregory of Nazianzus
Bishop of Constantinople (b. 329, d. 390)

I believe, O Lord, and I confess that You are truly the Christ, the son of the Living God, Who came into the world to save sinners, of whom I am the chief. And I believe that this is Your pure Body and Your own precious Blood. Therefore, I pray to You, have mercy on me and forgive my transgressions, voluntary and involuntary, in word and deed, known and unknown. And grant that I may partake of Your Holy Mysteries without condemnation, for the remission of sins and for life eternal. Amen.[7]

Saint John Chrysostom
Patriarch of Constantinople (b. *c.* 349, d. 407)

Imprint Christ . . . onto your heart, where he [already] dwells; whether you read a book about him, or behold him in an image, may he inspire your thoughts, as you come to know him twofold through the twofold experience of your senses. Thus you will see with your eyes what you have learned through the words you have heard. He who in this way hears and sees will fill his entire being with the praise of God.[8]

Saint Theodore the Studite
Byzantine monastic reformer (759–826)

JUDAS' KISS | *Mosaic, 6th century*

3

THE FATHERS OF THE WEST

Come therefore, Lord Jesus, to look for your servant, to search for the tired sheep. Come, O Shepherd, and look for me as Joseph sought his brethren (Gen 37:16). Your sheep has gone astray, while you dwelt in the mountains. Leave there the ninety-nine other sheep, and come after the one which strayed away. Come without the dogs, without the bad workers, without the hirelings too uncouth to enter through the door. Come without seeking help or being announced: long have I awaited your arrival. I know that you will come, "because I have not forgotten your commandments." Come, not with a whip, but with charity and gentleness of heart. . . . Come to me, for I am disturbed by the incursions of the ravening wolves. . . . Come to look for me, for I too am seeking you. Search for me, find me, gather me to you, carry me. You can find the one you seek: deign to welcome the one you find, and to place him on your shoulders. . . . Draw me to you in this flesh which failed in Adam; draw me to you, not from Sarah, but from Mary. . . . Carry me to your cross, which is the salvation of the lost and the only rest of the weary, to your cross by which whoever dies can live again.[1]

Saint Ambrose
Bishop of Milan (b. *c.* 339, d. 397)

He who but a short time before had cured the eyes of the blind man with His own spittle is now covered with the spittle of His persecutors. He who now crowns the martyrs with eternal garlands is now crowned with thorns. He who now gives true palms to the victors is beaten in the face with hostile palms. He who now clothes all others with the garment of immortality is stripped of His earthly garments. . . . The stars are stupefied by the crucifixion of the Lord, the elements disturbed, the earth shattered, night blots out the day. . . . All this time He does not speak, He does not proclaim His majesty. He endures all things, even to the bitter end, with constant perseverance so that in Him a full and perfect patience may find realization.[2]

Saint Cyprian
Bishop of Carthage (d. 258)

O wondrous power of the cross! O unspeakable glory of the passion which became the Lord's tribunal, the world's judgment, and the power of the Crucified! From Your cross You draw all things to Yourself, O Lord! When You stretched out Your hands to an unbelieving people that mocked You, the whole world was finally brought to confess Your majesty. . . . In this way type gave way to truth, prophecy to revelation, the ancient law to the gospel. You drew all things to Yourself, Lord, so that what previously was performed in the one temple of the Jews in mystic signs is now celebrated everywhere by holy men in every country in revealing rites. . . . Your cross is the font of all blessings, the source of all graces, and through it the believers receive strength in return for weakness, glory in return for shame, life in return for death.[3]

Pope Saint Leo the Great
(b. *c.* 400, d. 461)

There comes to my mind what the bystanders said derisively of the crucified Son of God: "If he is the king of Israel, let him come down from the cross, and we will believe him." If he had yielded to their derision, and come down then from the cross, he would not have demonstrated to us the virtue of patience. Instead, he waited for a while; he endured their taunts, he bore with their mockery, he preserved his patience, he deferred their esteem, and he who did not will to come down from the cross rose from the sepulcher.

Rising from the tomb was a greater thing than coming down from the cross. Destroying death by rising from the dead was a greater thing than preserving life by descending from the cross. When the bystanders saw that he was not coming down from the cross at their derisive remarks, when they saw him dying, they believed they had prevailed. They rejoiced as if they had consigned his name to oblivion. But see how his name has increased throughout the world, how the multitude which rejoiced over his slaying now grieves over his death! They perceive that it is through his suffering that Christ has arrived at glory.[4]

Pope Saint Gregory the Great
(b. *c.* 540, d. 604)

THE HEAVENLY JERUSALEM | *Liber Augustini de Civitate Dei*

4

SAINT AUGUSTINE

No book of prayers to Jesus Christ would be complete without a special section on Saint Augustine. Most of the Church Fathers did not write prayers formally, except, perhaps, liturgical prayers. We can look through their books without finding many direct prayers. The opposite is true of Saint Augustine. His works often include prayers, and his great *Confessions* is one long prayer to God the Father, to Christ, and, occasionally, to the Holy Spirit.

Augustine's prayers show his tremendous dedication to and dependence on Christ for the grace of salvation. He was deeply aware that he would have had no hope of salvation without Christ's direct intervention in his life. He clearly says that he was called by an unheard voice, that Christ was there for him.

From a Christian point of view, Augustine was perhaps the greatest mind since Saint Paul. The *Confessions*, a unique document, is the earliest psychological autobiography, giving us a man's inner experience. It has been said that there would not be another until 1600, when Cellini wrote his psychological autobiography.

Despite these distinctions, the most important thing for us is Augustine's prayerfulness and dedication to Christ. I have been reading his prayers since I was a teenager, and, except for the Scriptures, I have found them the greatest literary treasure I could imagine. I hope these prayers will give you further insight into the man and a desire to become familiar with his writings.

O food and bread of angels, the angels are filled by you, are satisfied by you, but not to the point of satiety. They live by you; they have wisdom by you. By you they are blessed. Where are you for my sake? In a mean lodging, in a manger. For whom? He who rules the stars sucks at the breast. He who speaks in the bosom of the Father is silent in the mother's lap. But he will speak when he reaches a suitable age, and will fulfill for us the gospel. For our sakes he will suffer, for us he will die. As an example of our reward, he will rise again. He will ascend into heaven before the eyes of his disciples, and he will come from heaven to judge the world. Behold him lying in the manger; he is reduced to tininess, yet he has not lost anything of himself. He has accepted what was not his, but he remains what he was. Look, we have the infant Christ; let us grow with him.[1]

And now, again, it is my Lord himself—who by his words has suddenly transported me from the weakness that was mine to the strength that was his—whom I hear saying, "Now my soul is troubled." What does that mean? How can you bid my soul follow you if I see your own soul troubled? How shall I endure what I feel to be so unendurably heavy? What kind of support can I seek if the rock itself gives way? But I think I hear in my own thoughts the Lord giving me an answer, saying, "You will follow me all the better, because it is to aid your powers of endurance that I bring myself to you this way. You have heard, as addressed to yourself, the voice of my strength; hear in me now the voice of your weakness. I supply the strength for your running your distance, and I do not stop your hastening along; but I do transfer to myself the causes for your trembling, and I pave the way for you to march along." O Lord our mediator, God above us, made man for us, I acknowledge your mercy! For because you, who are so great, are troubled through the good will of your love, you preserve in the richness of your comfort the many in your body who are troubled by the continual experience of their own weakness; preserve them from perishing utterly in their despair.[2]

That men might be born of God, God was first born of them. For Christ is God, and Christ was born of men. It was only a mother, indeed, that he sought upon earth, because he already had a father in heaven. He by whom we were to be created was born of God, and he by whom we were to be re-created was born of a woman. Marvel not, then, O man, that you are made a son by grace, that you are born of God according to his Word. The Word himself first chose to be born of man so that you might be born of God and into salvation, and say to yourself, Not without reason did God wish to be born of man, but because he counted me of some importance, that he might make me immortal and for my sake be born as a mortal man. When, therefore, he said, "born of God," because we might as a result be filled with amazement and tremble at such grace, a grace so great as to exceed belief that men are born of God, as if to reassure us, he also said, "And the Word was made flesh, and dwelt among us." Why, then, do you marvel that men are born of God? Remember simply, that God himself was born of men: "And the Word was made flesh, and dwelt among us."[3]

Fed with this simple and pure faith, fed as with milk, may we be nourished in Christ. As the little ones we are, let us not seek the food of our elders, but with the most wholesome nourishment grow in Christ, a good life and Christian righteousness being added to us, finding in them the love of God and of our neighbor perfected and confirmed, so that each one of us may triumph in himself over our enemy the devil and his fallen angels, through Christ whom we have put on. Perfect love has neither the desire to obtain purely temporal things nor the fear of losing those temporal things. By those two doors our enemy enters in and reigns, an enemy we must drive out, first by the fear of God and next by love. We ought, therefore, all the more eagerly to seek an open and clear knowledge of the truth the more we find ourselves making progress in love, and in its simplicity feel our hearts purified, for it is with our inner eyes that we see the truth, for as we know, "Blessed are the pure in heart, for they shall see God." Rooted and grounded in love, we may be able to comprehend with the saints the true breadth and length and height and depth of things, knowing also that love of Christ which passes knowledge, so that we may be filled with the fullness of God. We hope, then, after these contests with our unseen enemy, we may win the crown of victory, since to those who are willing and who truly love, the yoke of Christ is easy and his burden light.[4]

The blind man cried out as Christ was passing by, for he feared that Christ would pass without curing him. And how did he cry? He cried so that he would not be silenced by the crowd. He triumphed over its opposition and won his Saviour. In spite of the crowd who strove to silence the blind

man, Jesus stood still, and called to him, and said, "What wilt
thou that I do?" "Lord," he said, "that I may see." And Our
Lord answered, "Receive thy sight: thy faith hath made thee
whole." Have a love for Christ; desire the light, which is
Christ. If that blind man desired the light of the body, how
much more should you desire the light in your heart. Let us
cry out to Him, not with our voices, but with our works. Let
us live holy lives and despise the world; let all transitory things
be as nothing to us. Worldly men, when they see us living in
this fashion, will give us, as they deem it, a friendly warning.
They love the world and the things of dust, without a
thought of heaven, and take freely what enjoyment they can
find. They will surely censure us if they see us despising these
things of earth. They will say, "What mad thing are you
doing?" They form the censuring crowd who want to pre-
vent the blind man from crying out. There are some Christians who are against a Christian mode of life, for that crowd
itself was walking with Christ, and impeding a blind man
who was crying out with all his might for Christ, and wishing
for the light from the succour of Christ. There are some
Christians of this kind, but let us conquer them by our holy
lives, and let our life itself cry out to Christ. He will stand for
us, because He stands for ever (*stabit, quia stat*).

For there is a great mystery in this. [Christ] was passing by
when the blind man cried out, but when He healed He stood
still. Let this passing by of Christ make us eager to cry to
Him. What is the passing by of Christ? Whatever He bore for
us in time constitutes His passing. He was born: in this He
has passed, for is He still being born? He grew: in this He has
passed, for does He still grow? He was at His mother's breast,
and does He still suck? When He was weary He slept; does
He still sleep? Last of all He was taken and loaded with
chains, scourged, crowned with thorns, struck, and spit upon,

hung upon a tree, put to death, pierced by a lance, and He rose again from the sepulchre; He is still passing. He ascended into Heaven, and sits at the right hand of the Father; that is His permanent place. Cry to Him as much as you can; He will now enlighten you; for inasmuch as "the Word was with God," He did not pass by, for He was the unchangeable God. And "the Word was God, and the Word was made flesh." In His human passing the flesh did and suffered many things; the Word was immutable. The heart is enlightened in that Word itself, because in that Word itself the flesh which He took upon Himself is honoured. Take away the Word, and what is the flesh? Nothing more than the flesh of any ordinary man. "But the Word was made flesh and dwelt amongst us," that the flesh of Christ might be honoured. Let us therefore cry out to Him and live holy lives.[5]

Saint Augustine of Hippo
(354–430)

5

THE DARK AGES

The Dark Ages refer to the turbulent times following the collapse of the Roman Empire in the West up to the medieval period—approximately five hundred years. With the collapse of the empire and the invasion of barbarian tribes, civilization took a step back in many ways. However, many historians dispute whether the period was as dark as it is sometimes described. The interpretation of these centuries may be the result of some historical prejudices.

During the Dark Ages many great things happened, among them the spread of the Order of Saint Benedict, which brought education, enlightenment, medical services, and an extremely powerful liturgical piety throughout western Europe. It can truly be said that Europe has lived on the foundation laid by the Benedictine monks.

The piety of this time was largely biblical and liturgical, because in turbulent times people apparently did not spend much time on their inner feelings or desires. They related to Christ and to God very much as the great King and His Son. People of our time, who are so psychologized, find it difficult to understand the people of those ages. It might be easier for people growing up in the Third World (rather than in what we presumptively call the First World) to understand them.

It is interesting to note that the Dark Ages survived; they became the medieval times. The very architecture that characterized those ages became the beautiful Gothic architecture of the medieval cathedrals.

If you are attracted to liturgical prayer, you should know that much of the liturgical tradition is related to the monks, especially at the end of the period.

PORTRAIT OF CHRIST | *Book of Kells, circa 800*

I arise today
Through a mighty strength,
the invocation of the Trinity,
Through belief in the threeness,
Through confession of the oneness
Of the Creator of Creation.

I arise today
Through the strength of Christ's birth
   with His baptism,
Through the strength of His crucifixion
   with His burial,
Through the strength of His resurrection
   with His ascension,
Through the strength of His coming down for Judgement.

Christ to shield me this day,
So that there come to me abundance of reward.
Christ with me, Christ before me, Christ behind me,
Christ in me, Christ beneath me, Christ above me,
Christ when I lie down, Christ when I sit,
Christ when I arise,
Christ in the heart of every man who thinks of me,
Christ in the mouth of everyone who speaks of me,
Christ in every eye that sees me,
Christ in every ear that hears me.[1]

Saint Patrick
Missionary apostle to Ireland (b. *c.* 389, d. *c.* 461)

The regal dark mysterious cross
  In song is lifted high,
The wood on which our God was raised
As Man against the sky.

Upon this wood his body bore
The nails, the taunts, the spear,
Till water flowed with blood to wash
The whole world free of fear.

At last the song that David sang
Is heard and understood:
"Before the nations God as king
Reigns from his throne of wood."

This wood now spread with purple wears
The pageantry of kings;
Of chosen stock it dares to hold
On high his tortured limbs.

O blessed Tree, upon whose arms
The world's own ransom hung;
His body pays our debt and life
From Satan's grasp is wrung.

O sacred Cross, our steadfast hope
In this our Passiontide,
Through you the Son obtained for all
Forgiveness as he died.

May every living creature praise
Our God both one and three,
Who rules in everlasting peace
All whom his cross makes free.[2]

Venantius Fortunatus
Poet, Bishop of Poitiers (b. *c.* 540, d. *c.* 600)

O King of Kings,
    O sheltering wings, O guardian tree!
All, all of me,
Thou Virgin's nurseling, rests in thee.[3]

Ancient Irish poem

O holy Jesus; O gentle friend; O Morning Star; O mid-day Sun adorned. . . . For the sake of thy kindliness (affection, love, mercy) hear the entreaty of this man and wretched poorling and weakling for the acceptance of this sacrifice on behalf of all Christian churches, and on mine own behalf.[4]

Anonymous
(seventh or eighth century)

A nd I pray Thee, loving Jesus, that as Thou hast graciously given me to drink in with delight the words of Thy knowledge, so Thou wouldst mercifully grant me to attain one day to Thee, the fountain of all wisdom and to appear forever before Thy face.[5]

Venerable Bede
(672–735)

The time is right and I repent
  every trespass, O my Lord.
Pardon me my every crime,
Christ, as Thou art merciful.

By Thy incarnation sweet,
by Thy birth, my sacred King,
by Thy lasting baptism here,
pardon me my every wrong.

By Thy hanging, filled with love,
by Thy rising from the dead,
all my passions pardon me,
Lord who art truly merciful.

By Thy ascension—glorious hour—
to holy Heaven, to the Father
(promised ere Thou didst depart)
pardon me my every wrong.

By Thy coming holy word
to judge the hosts of Adam's seed,
by heaven's orders nine revealed
be my offence forgiven me.

By the ranks of profit true,
by the martyrs' worthy throng,
by the train of noble Fathers,
pardon the crimes that mastered me.

By the band of the pure apostles,
by the chaste disciples' host,

by each saint of royal favor,
pardon me my evil deeds.

Lord, O Lord, hear me,
Fill my soul, Lord, with Thy love's ray,
Fill my soul, Lord, with Thy love's ray,
Lord, O Lord, hear me.[6]

Saint Oengus
Irish monastic reformer (eighth century)

Hunger and thirst, O Christ, for sight of Thee,
Came between me and all the fears of earth.
Give Thou Thyself the Bread, Thyself the Wine,
Thou, sole provision for the unknown way.
Long hunger wasted the world wanderer,
With sight of Thee may he be satisfied.[7]

Saint Radbod
Bishop of Utrecht (b. *c.* 850, d. 917)

Long ago was it that I was cut down at the edge of the forest, moved from my trunk. Men bore me on their shoulders, they set me on a hill. I saw then the Lord of mankind hasten with great zeal that He might be raised upon me.

"Then the young Hero—He was God almighty—firm and unflinching, stripped Himself; He mounted on the high cross, brave in the sight of many, when He was minded to redeem mankind. Then I trembled when the Hero clasped me; yet I durst not bow to the earth, fall to the level of the ground, but I must needs stand firm.

"As a rood was I raised up; I bore aloft the mighty King, the Lord of heaven. They pierced me with dark nails; the wounds are still plain to view in me, gaping gashes of malice. I was all bedewed with blood, shed from the Man's side, after He had sent forth His Spirit. I saw the God of hosts violently stretched out. All creation wept, lamented the King's death; Christ was on the cross.

"Now the time has come when far and wide over the earth and all this splendid creation, men do me honor; they worship this sign. On me the Son of God suffered for a space; wherefore now I rise glorious beneath the heavens, and I can heal all who fear me.

"Now I bid thee, my loved man, to declare this vision unto men; reveal in words that it is the glorious tree on which Almighty God suffered for the sins of mankind and the old deeds of Adam. . . ."

Then glad at heart, I worshipped the cross with great zeal. Now I have joy of life that I can seek the triumphant cross, do it full honor. Great is the desire for that in my heart, and to the cross I turn for help. May the Lord, who here on earth suffered aforetime on the cross for the sins of men, be a friend unto me; He has redeemed us and has given us life, a heavenly home.[8]

The Dream of the Rood
Poem written in Old English (eighth century)

6

THE EARLY MIDDLE AGES

One of the more beautiful and remarkable periods of European history is the beginning of the medieval period, from about the ninth century to the time of Saint Francis. The rather chaotic world of the barbarian kingdoms was being organized on Christian values and kingdoms. Charlemagne brought law and order and education to various parts of northern Europe.

Again, at this time, the Benedictines and, later, the Cistercian reformers were powerful in shaping the Church's prayer life. Here and there figures emerged who would have a lasting effect on the intellectual and prayer life of western Europe—men such as Alcuin of York and the reforming Benedictine abbot John of Fécamp, who was among the first writers to bring affective devotion to his meditations. For the first time, people began to pray frequently to Christ crucified. This was an interesting development, because everyone knew that in heaven Christ was not crucified. How can you pray to Christ crucified now? The answer is that we remember His sufferings, we live through them in our mind, and we speak to Him as if His sufferings were present, even though we know that at this moment He is the glorious victor in eternal life.

Prayer to Jesus crucified is one of the great marks of medieval piety. Jesus, Mary, the apostles and the saints became living figures to medieval people, who began to think more about how people felt. The piety of remembrance—the Child Jesus, the Good Shepherd walking the fields of Galilee, the crucified Son of God, the resurrected Christ—marked the piety of the people who saw the beginning of the modern world—the medieval times.

FLAGELLATION AND CRUCIFIXION | *Stadtkirche, Esslingen, Germany*

Adore the lifted standard of the Cross,
O faithful soul.
Who takes it for his sign, need fear no sorrow.
That blessed cross, where the Lord's body hung,
And by his dying, closed the road to death.
   He that created life, slew death by dying,
   And by his wounds are the world's wounds made whole.[1]

He lay with quiet heart in the stern asleep:
Waking, commanded both the winds and sea.
Christ, though this weary body slumber deep,
   Grant that my heart may keep its watch with thee.
O Lamb of God that carried all our sin,
   Guard thou my sleep against the enemy.[2]

Lord Christ, we pray thy mercy on our table spread,
And what thy gentle hands have given thy men
Let it by thee be blessed: whate'er we have
Came from thy lavish heart and gentle hand,
And all that's good is thine, for thou art good.
And ye that eat, give thanks for it to Christ,
And let the words ye utter be only peace,
For Christ loved peace: it was himself that said,
Peace I give unto you, my peace I leave with you.
Grant that our own may be a generous hand
Breaking the bread for all poor men, sharing the food.
Christ shall receive the bread thou gavest his poor,
And shall not tarry to give thee reward.[3]

Alcuin of York
Master of the palace school at the court of Charlemagne
(b. *c.* 735, d. 804)

Lord Jesus Christ, for the sake of Thy holy Cross, be with me to shield me. Amen.

Lord Jesus Christ, by the memory of Thy blessed Cross, be within me to strengthen me. Amen.

Lord Jesus Christ, for Thy holy Cross, be ever round about me to protect me. Amen.

Lord Jesus Christ, for Thy glorious Cross, go before me to direct my steps. Amen.

Lord Jesus Christ, for Thy adorable Cross, come Thou after me to guard me. Amen.

Lord Jesus Christ, for Thy Cross, worthy of all praise, overshadow me to bless me. Amen.

Lord Jesus Christ, for Thy noble Cross, be Thou in me to lead me to Thy kingdom. Amen.[4]

Seven Petitions to the Holy Cross

May the power of Thy holy Cross, I beseech Thee, O Lord, go before me and lead me through the day, wheresoever I may be. In Thy mercy so guide me to-day that my enemy may find in me nothing that is his, but all that is Thine; or, should aught of evil be so found by reason of my frailty, may Thy loving kindness quickly blot it out. May Thy holy angel guard me and bring me safe and unharmed unto the evening hour. Amen.

O Christ, who hast bought us with Thy precious blood, save us who adore Thee as our God. Do Thou save us, who didst suffer for us hanging on the Cross. With that Cross we sign our foreheads and hearts, venerating Thee and this same holy sign, and begging that by its power Thou wilt shield us and protect us all the days of our life, and, snatching us from the fires of hell, wilt bestow on us the joys of the eternal resurrection. . . .

O Redeemer of the world, by this sign of the Cross guard us from all evil chances. Thou who didst save Peter on the sea, have mercy on us.[5]

Early Morning Offerings

Jesus Christ, the beginning and the end, the resurrection and the life, the perfect man who gave his life for sinners, I worship you, I adore you, I sing aloud your name. I am one of those whom you saved, whom you set free, when you died on the cross. You redeemed me from the slavery of sin. And yet I cannot escape the over-powering sense that I am still a wretched sinner, that my every action is worthless or evil. I am like the dry sand of a desert thirsting for water. I am like a criminal languishing in prison. Good people try to help me, and I pray that you will reward them; but their goodness does nothing to assuage my sense of wickedness. Patient people try to teach me your ways; but I am so stubborn that I cannot learn. Humble people seek to serve me; but in my pride I cannot truly appreciate their services. Lift the burden of wickedness; break down my stubbornness; root out my pride. Let me receive your life-giving love. Let me be free.[6]

Saint Fulbert
Bishop of Chartres (b. *c.* 970, d. 1028)

Lord Jesus Christ,
I approach your banquet table
in fear and trembling,
for I am a sinner,
and dare not rely on my own worth
but only on your goodness and mercy. . . .
Praise to you, saving sacrifice,
offered on the wood of the cross for me and for all
    mankind.
Praise to the noble and precious blood,
flowing from the wounds of my crucified Lord Jesus Christ
and washing away the sins of the whole world.
Remember, Lord, your creature,
whom you have redeemed with your blood.[7]

John of Fécamp
(1028–1078)

CRUCIFIXION | *Andreas Missal, circa 1320*

7

THE MONKS

From the collapse of the Roman Empire in the fifth century and during the ensuing barbarian invasions, it was the monks who kept Europe alive. Western Europe owes its existence as a unit of human civilization to the Order of Saint Benedict. It was, in fact, a Benedictine monk, Saint Gregory the Great, who took over management of the empire when the emperor fled before the barbarian hordes. For the next five hundred years, much of the Church's life in the West was fashioned by the monks and their prayers. We have already met with some of the monks, but we must pay special recognition to some of the outstanding monks and their gift to Christian civilization at the end of the Dark Ages.

We include Saint Anselm, philosopher and theologian, a man of warm personal devotion to Jesus Christ. Saint Bernard belonged to the Cistercian abbey of Clairvaux, an eleventh-century reform of the Benedictines, and was in many ways the first modern Christian. He was especially drawn to contemplate Jesus crucified through the events of his life, and he was not ashamed to express his devotion in a most human, even emotional, way. No doubt many people praying fervently to Christ in modern times have failed to recognize how much they owe to the reforming abbot of Clairvaux.

Similar things may be said of Aelred of Rievaulx and William of Saint-Thierry, both of whom were theological writers of insight and monks of the reformed Benedictine tradition of Cîteaux. The eleventh and twelfth centuries were a time of growth, a "second spring" for monastic life and for

the Church, after the darkness of the earlier centuries. Benedictines, especially those of the Cluniac and Cistercian re-
forms, did a great deal to define the Church's life in the
future. It would come as a surprise to many to realize that
many of the customs we observe at Mass today were begun
by monks at the end of the Dark Ages.

The name of Jesus is more than light, it is also food. Do you not feel increase of strength as often as you remember it? What other name can so enrich the man who meditates? What can equal its power to refresh the harassed senses, to buttress the virtues, to add vigor to good and upright habits, to foster chaste affections? . . . Write what you will, I shall not relish it unless it tells of Jesus. Talk or argue about what you will, I shall not relish it if you exclude the name of Jesus. Jesus to me is honey in the mouth, music in the ear, a song in the heart.

Again, it is a medicine. Does one of us feel sad? Let the name of Jesus come into his heart, from there let it spring to his mouth, so that shining like the dawn it may dispel all darkness and make a cloudless sky. Does someone fall into sin? Does his despair even urge him to suicide? Let him but invoke this life-giving name and his will to live will be at once renewed.[1]

The infant Christ does not console the talkative; the tears of Christ do not console those who rejoice in worldly things; his swaddling clothes do not console those who are clad in rich garments; the stable and the manger do not console those who love the front seats in the synagogue; but perhaps they will one day see that this universal consolation descends on those who await the Lord in silence, those who weep, those who are dressed in poor clothes.[2]

Saint Bernard of Clairvaux
(1090–1153)

As much as I can, though not as much as I ought, I am mindful of your passion, your buffeting, your scourging, your cross, your wounds, how you were slain for me, how prepared for burial and buried. . . . And I also remember your glorious resurrection, and wonderful ascension. . . . Why, O my soul, were you not there to be pierced by a sword of bitter sorrow when you could not bear the piercing of the side of your Savior with a lance? Why could you not bear to see the nails violate the hands and feet of your creator? . . . Why did you not share the sufferings of the most pure virgin, his worthy mother and your gentle lady? . . . Would that I with happy Joseph might have taken down my Lord from the cross, wrapped him in spiced grave-clothes, and laid him in the tomb. Would that with the blessed band of women I might have trembled at the vision of angels and have heard the news of the Lord's resurrection.[3]

Who will snatch me from the hands of God?
Who shall be my help, my salvation?
Who is the one called "the angel of great counsel,"
the one called savior, that I may call upon his name?
It is Jesus, yes, Jesus himself.
He is the judge between whose hands I tremble.
But breathe now a sigh of relief, O sinner,
yes, breathe a sigh of relief, and do not despair.
Hope in him whom you fear.
Flee to him from whom you fled.
Insistently invoke the one whom your pride provoked.
Jesus, Jesus, because of that name treat me according to
    that name.

Jesus, Jesus, ignore the proud man who provokes you,
see only the wretched one who invokes you.
Sweet name! Name full of delights!
Name that comforts sinners and brings them blessed hope.
For what is Jesus if not savior?
Therefore, Jesus, because of who you are, be Jesus for me.
You who fashioned me, let me not perish.
You who redeemed me, let me not be condemned. . . .
If you let me into the wide embrace of your mercy,
it will not be narrowed because of me, O Lord,
Admit me therefore, O dearest Jesus,
admit me among the number of your elect,
so that with them I may praise you, enjoy you,
    and glory in you.[4]

Saint Anselm
Archbishop of Canterbury (b. 1033, d. 1109)

When we look more closely at the picture of your passion, although it does not speak, we seem to hear you say: "When I loved you, I loved you to the end. Let death and hell lay hold on me, that I may die their death; eat, friends, and drink abundantly, beloved, unto life eternal."

For through this picturing of your passion, O Christ, our pondering on the good that you have wrought for us leads us forthwith to love the highest good. That good you make us see in the work of salvation, not by an understanding arising from human effort nor by the eyes of our mind that tremble and shrink from your light, but by the peaceful experience of love, and by the good use of our sight and enjoyment of your sweetness, while your wisdom sweetly orders our affairs. For he labors who would go up some other way, but he who enters by you, O Door, walks on the smooth ground and comes to the Father. . . . [A]s the river of joy floods that soul more completely, she seems to see you as you are. In sweet meditation on the wonderful sacrament of your passion she muses on the good that you have wrought on our behalf, the good that is as great as you yourself are great, the good that is yourself. She seems to herself to see you face to face when you thus show her, in the cross and in the work of your salvation, the face of the ultimate Good. The cross itself becomes for her the face of a mind that is well-disposed toward God.[5]

William of Saint-Thierry
(1085–1148)

W ho will give me wings, as of a dove, that I may fly, and find rest? Till then let my soul be fledged, Lord Jesus, let it grow wings, I pray You, in the nest of your chastening: let it rest in the cleft of the rock, in the cavern of Your wounds. Let it embrace You, the crucified one: let it take from You the draught of Your precious blood. While I wait, let this sweet meditation fill my memory, lest forgetfulness darken it for me: while I wait, let me look upon myself as knowing nothing, except my Lord, and Him crucified, lest empty error seduce my knowledge from the firm foundation of the Faith, let the delight of all my love be in You, lest I be taken up by any worldly desire.[6]

Saint Aelred of Rievaulx
(1109–1167)

SAINT FRANCIS OF ASSISI | *El Greco (1541–1614)*

8

THE FRIARS

With Saints Francis and Dominic, religious life took an important turn. It was no longer based on seclusion, the daily observance of long offices, and the construction of a beautiful abbey, which represented on earth a symbol of the heavenly Jerusalem. The friars were the monks in the street and among the people, and the friars' movement, which included orders such as the Augustinians, the Carmelites, and the Servites, was the beginning of a real amalgamation of popular piety and religious life.

The prayers of the friars and the second-order nuns associated with their communities, such as the Poor Clares, as well as the piety of the lay third-order members, or tertiaries, were much more personal and psychologically sensitive than the prayers of the Dark Ages. Readers who grew up with the traditional Catholic piety of the past may recognize that much of it was derived from the friars, although many elements came also from the Catholic Reformation period.

Saint Francis and the other friars were responsible for preaching and spreading devotion among the faithful to Jesus crucified, to His Passion, to the Child Jesus born in the manger and crucified in agony. The popularity of Marian devotion, although it began with the monks, came to flower at this time.

Although we do not have examples of the prayers of many important saints from this time, we do have a marvelous selection of the warm, affectionate prayers of Saint Francis. Spiritually, he is a towering figure of the devotion of the early Middle Ages. His popularity through the centuries is based on the fact that he could express an experience of religious devotion that most people could understand. Apparently for different reasons generation after generation has found great meaning in Saint Francis' piety and in the sincerity with which he lived out that piety.

All-powerful, most holy,
Almighty and supreme God,
Holy and just *Father,*
Lord King *of heaven and earth*
we thank You for Yourself
for through Your holy will
and through Your only Son
with the Holy Spirit
You have created everything spiritual and corporal
and, after making us *in Your own image and likeness,*
You placed us in paradise.
Through our own fault we fell.
We thank You
For as through Your Son You created us,
So through Your holy love
With which You loved us
You brought about His birth
As true God and true man
By the glorious, ever-virgin, most blessed, holy Mary
and You willed to redeem us captives
through His cross and blood and death.
Because all of us, wretches and sinners,
Are not worthy to pronounce Your name,
We humbly ask Our Lord Jesus Christ,
Your *beloved Son,*
in Whom You were well pleased,
together with the Holy Spirit,
the Paraclete,
to give You thanks, for everything
as it pleases You and Him,
Who always satisfies You in everything,
through Whom You have done so much for us.
Alleluia![1]

Let all of us, brothers, consider the Good Shepherd Who bore the suffering of the cross to save His sheep.

The Lord's sheep followed Him in tribulation and persecution, shame and hunger, in weakness and temptation, and in other ways; and for these things they received eternal life from the Lord.

Therefore, it is a great shame for us, the servants of God, that the saints have accomplished great things and we want only to receive glory and honor by recounting them.[2]

Lord Jesus Christ,
who chose the twelve Apostles,
and though one of them was lost,
the rest remained true to you
and preached the Gospel,
being filled with the Holy Spirit:
now, Lord, in your mercy
you have endowed the brothers with faith
so that they can strengthen others
and so fulfill the mystery of the Gospel.
Who, then, can make satisfaction
when the very ones whom you have sent
do not bear witness to the light
but instead do the works of darkness?[3]

My Lord Jesus Christ,
I thank you
for the great love and charity
you show me.
For it is a sign of great love
when the Lord punishes his servant
for all his misdeeds in this world
rather than punish him in the next.
And I am joyfully prepared
to undergo every trial
and every adversity which you, God,
are pleased to send me
for my sins.[4]

Lord Jesus Christ,
you are the good shepherd.
You grant us
your loving mercy
without our having deserved it,
and many a time it must endure the pangs of sharp pain.
Since you have called me to your flock,
I beg you by your grace and strength
that in trouble, anguish and distress
I may never turn away from you.
Lord, look down on me in my infirmities
and help me to bear them patiently.[5]

Saint Francis of Assisi
(1182–1226)

We ask You, Lord Jesus,
that You be a Good Shepherd for us,
guard us, Your flock,
defend us from the hired hand and the wolf,
and crown us with the crown
of eternal life in Your Kingdom.
You who are blessed, glorious, and praiseworthy
Throughout all ages.
May every stray sheep and
Every faithful soul answer: "Amen. Alleluia!"[6]

O sweet Jesus! Who is sweeter than You?
Your memory is sweeter than honey,
A name of sweetness, a name of salvation.
What does the name "Jesus" mean, if not a Savior?
Good Jesus, therefore, be a "Jesus" for us.
You who are the source of sweetness,
that is, of faith, give us hope and charity,
that, living and dying in it,
we may merit to come to You.
This we ask, with Your help,
And the prayers of Your Mother,
You who are blessed forever and ever. Amen.[7]

Lord Jesus, may You be loyal to the covenant
You ratified with Your blood for Your children.
May we not fall prey to the evil one.
Do not abandon the souls of Your servants,
which You have redeemed,
who apart from You have nothing to hope for.
You who are blessed and glorious for all ages. Amen.[8]

Follow me!" Jesus said to Peter, and today He repeats these same words to every Christian. . . .

In the third chapter of Jeremiah, we read, "You will call me 'My Father' and never cease to follow me" (3:19). Follow me, then, by casting aside anything that weighs you down, for if you are thus burdened, you will not be able to keep up with me since I am running in haste.

In the words of the psalmist: Christ says, "I ran in thirst" (61:5; DRV), thirst for the salvation of all. Where did he run? To the Cross! You too should run after Him, carrying your cross after Him who so eagerly carried His Cross for you. . . .

"Follow me" for I know where to take you. The Book of Proverbs says, "On the way of wisdom I direct you, I lead you on straightforward paths" (4:11). . . .

The way of wisdom is the way of humility: every other way is that of ignorance and pride. Jesus showed us the way of wisdom when he said, "Learn from me" (Mt 11:29). When we follow Christ, who guides us by His example, we walk a very narrow path, a path of poverty and obedience. . . .

Although obedience and poverty seem to confine and restrict our freedom, nevertheless, poverty makes us rich, and obedience makes us free. Whoever follows Jesus along the straight and narrow path will not be hampered by attachment to riches and to his own will.[9]

Saint Anthony of Padua
(b. *c.* 1195, d. 1231)

VISION OF SAINT THOMAS AQUINAS | *Stefano di Giovanni (d. 1450)*

9

THE MEDIEVAL THEOLOGIANS

Along with figures such as Saints Dominic and Francis, the later medieval times gave rise to some outstanding theological minds. Preeminent among them were Saints Thomas Aquinas, a Dominican, and Bonaventure, a Franciscan, and there are many others. Their piety, although profoundly theological and expressing their opinions about theological controversies of the times, has come down to us in the form of popular hymns and prayers.

The hymns of Saint Thomas, which are still sung at Benediction and at Eucharistic celebrations, were familiar to Catholics, until a few generations ago, in their original Latin. We should meditate on the immensely rich prayers of the medieval theologians and recognize that they are profoundly scriptural and based very much on Gospel and other New Testament images.

Lord Jesus Christ, listen to the voice of our distress in the desert of penitents crying out to you; that we may not be deceived by the falsehood of discussions in nobility of birth, from superstition of religion, from curiosity of knowledge tempting us; grant us to prepare the way to you by abandoning sin, by the purpose of repenting, by the remission of wrongs, by contempt of temporal [things], and by the observing of the commandments. May your paths be made straight in us by the renunciation of our own will, feeling, self-confidence, by the spending over and above of counsels/deliberations; that in the house of Bethany of obedience baptized with the water of true contrition, with the Holy Spirit and with fire across the Jordan, and after the river of the last judgment we may perfectly know you, the Mediator of virtue and knowledge, the Mediator of God and men.[1]

Saint Albert the Great
(1206–1280)

Thus do thou distinguish the steps that lead to the way
    of union:
let vigilance make thee attentive,
    for the Bridegroom passeth swiftly;
let confidence make thee strong,
    for he cometh without fail;
let desire enkindle thee,
    for he is sweet;
let fervour raise thee up,
    for he is sublime;
let delight in him give thee repose,
    for he is beautiful;
let joy inebriate thee,
    for he is the fullness of love;
let attachment unite thee to him,
    for his love is full of power.
And mayest thou ever, O devout soul, say to the Lord with
all thy heart:
    I seek thee,
    I hope for thee,
    I desire thee,
    I raise myself up toward thee,
    I lay hold on thee,
    I exult in thee,
    at last I cleave to thee.[2]

Pierce, O most sweet Lord Jesus, my inmost soul with the most joyous and healthful wound of Thy love, with true, serene, and most holy apostolic charity, that my soul may ever languish and melt with love and longing for Thee, that it may yearn for Thee and faint for Thy courts, and long to be dissolved and to be with Thee. Grant that my soul may hunger after Thee, the bread of angels, the refreshment of holy souls, our daily and supersubstantial bread, having all sweetness and savour and every delight of taste; let my heart ever hunger after and feed upon Thee, upon whom the angels desire to look, and may my inmost soul be filled with the sweetness of Thy savour; may it ever thirst after Thee, the fountain of life, the fountain of wisdom and knowledge, the fountain of eternal light, the torrent of pleasure, the richness of the house of God; may it ever compass Thee, seek Thee, find Thee, run to Thee, attain to Thee, meditate upon Thee, speak of Thee, and do all things to the praise and glory of Thy name with humility and discretion, with love and delight, with ease and affection, and with perseverance unto the end; mayest Thou alone be ever my hope, my entire assurance, my riches, my delight, my pleasure, my joy, my rest and tranquillity, my peace, my sweetness, my fragrance, my sweet savour, my food, my refreshment, my refuge, my help, my wisdom, my portion, my possession, and my treasure in whom may my mind and my heart be fixed and firm and rooted immovably henceforth and forever. Amen.

Saint Bonaventure
(1221–1274)

The Word from heaven now proceeding,
His Father's right hand never leaving,
Advancing to His proper work,
Approached His life's final evening.

By His disciple unto death
And soon by foes to be betrayed,
But first as life's true sustenance
To apostles He Himself conveyed.

To them beneath a twofold guise
He Flesh and Blood distributed;
Thus in corporeal substances
The entire man He justly fed.

Being born, He became our friend.
At supper, He became our food.
Dying, He paid our ransom's price
And reigning, gives eternal good.

O Sacrifice for our salvation,
Who Gate of Heaven opens wide,
Our enemies press hard around us.
Assist us strongly, be our guide.

To the One and Triune God,
Be glory and eternal praise.
May He grant us life forever
And to our home our souls upraise.[3]

With my heart I worship,
　　O hidden Deity,
Thou that dost hide Thyself
　　Beneath these images
　　　In full reality.

My heart submits to Thee,
　　Yea, all my thought:
For contemplating Thee,
　　All else is naught.

I cannot touch, I cannot taste, I cannot see.
　　All sense is cheated of Thee, but the ear.
The son of God hath spoken: I believe:
　　For naught hath truth beyond the word I hear.

Upon the cross Thy Deity was hid,
　　And here is hidden Thy humanity:
Yet here I do acknowledge both and cry,
　　As the thief cried to Thee on Calvary.

I do not gaze, like Thomas, on Thy wounds,
　　But I confess Thee God.
Give me a stronger faith, a surer hope,
　　More love to Thee, my Lord.

O thou memorial of the dying Lord,
　　O living Bread that givest life to men,
Make strong my soul that it may live by Thee,
　　And for all sweetness turn to Thee again.

O Christ that gave Thy heart to feed Thy young,
   Cleanse Thou my foulness in Thy blood was spilt.
One single drop of it would save a world,
   A whole world from its guilt.

The veil is on Thy face: I cannot see.
   I cry to Thee for grace,
That that may come to pass for which I thirst,
   That I may see Thee with Thy face unveiled,
     And in that vision rest.[4]

O God, who in this wonderful sacrament hast left us a memorial of Thy passion, grant us, we beseech Thee, so to venerate the sacred mysteries of Thy Body and Blood that we may ever perceive within us the fruit of Thy redemption.

Collect from the Mass of Corpus Christi

Saint Thomas Aquinas
(1225–1274)

I. Q uod corda fidelui tunent & uene xvi.
ari debet magnitudine. larutu
dine. altitudine timoru dni.

II. Q uod omni fidelis anima sapient xvii.
tunent dm. p fide sedes dm e.

III. Q uod pfunditas misteriorum dei xviii.
hominibz. incompensibilis e. n qm
tu ipso donante fide concipit.

IIII. Q d in sapientia di patris. p amo
re filiu siu pfectio omium elec
toru computata e.

V. Q xemplu ineuglio de eade re.

VI. Q d significet luceus um ipecto
re. & cur homo ab anglo nspernt.

VII. V erba ysaie ad eande re. nat.

VIII. V erba dauid.

VIIII. Q d ds pat insilio sio abatutora
uirgine incarnato. opat ordi
nat. ac pfiett omia opa sua.

X. D e circulo gtante.

XI. Q d potestas dn atuor e qm homi
nisciendu sit. & cur angli lau
dent dm.

XII. Q uod ds e pspicua iusticia. uer
& iustus absq; comutatione.

XIII. Q d iurtui iusticia. & iudiciu di nul
lum finem habet. qui cophendi pos
sit humano sensu.

XIIII. D e casu pim anglu & sibi ostentu
tibz. & qre. & quom. & q ocideru.

XV. V erba ezechielis de eadem re.

XVI. Q d gla splendoris illi que diabo
lus p supbia pdidit. seruata e ise
creto patris alt fadi luce.

XVII. Q d diabolus cecidit absq; herede.
homo aut cecidit habens herede.

XVIII. E xemplu de goliath & de dauid
ad eandem rem.

GOD ENTHRONED ON MAN'S FAITH | *Codex Rupertsberg, 12th century*

THE MYSTICS

Many of the people about whom we have spoken in this prayer book are mystics, that is, people who, regardless of their vocation, were favored with experiences of God far beyond the ordinary. We speak about genuine mysticism, about those who have seen and heard the sights and sounds of another world. Unfortunately, the word *mystic* is often abused.

Among the great mystics of the Middle Ages and the beginning of the Renaissance are a number of women. Outstanding among these is Saint Catherine of Siena, a laywoman who belonged to the Third Order of Saint Dominic. Catherine and other women mystics of the time, some religious and some lay (such as Julian of Norwich), lived lives of devout piety and Christian observance. Their writings were often unknown until after their death.

A number of the writers given here, such as the fourteenth-century English mystics, are not canonized saints, Some people believe that the English mystics, because of their saintly and edifying lives, would have been canonized save for the cataclysm of the Reformation. Whereas Walter Hilton was an Augustinian prior, Richard Rolle and Julian of Norwich were both anchorites, or hermits.

We can learn much from the complete trust in God and the absolute consecration of life reflected in the writings of the mystics.

Lord, the woman fallen in many sins, seeing Thy
    Divinity,
Taking the part of myrrh-bearer, wailing bringeth to Thee
    myrrh against Thy burial;
"Alas!" she crieth, "for that night is to me the wilderness of
    sin, dusky and moonless, even the love of transgression;
Accept the springs of my tears, who with clouds partest the
    waters of the sea;
Bend to the groanings of my heart, who hast brought down
    Heaven by Thine ineffable humiliation:
I will kiss again Thy stainless feet,
I will wipe them with the hair of my head;
Thy feet, whereof when Eve in Paradise heard the sound,
    she hid herself for fear;
The multitude of my sins, and the depths of Thy judgment,
    who shall explore, Saviour of souls, my Redeemer?
Forget not me, Thy servant, Thou, whose mercy is
    infinite!" [1]

Saint Cassiane
Byzantine nun (ninth century)

Jesus Christ, the love that gives love,
    You are higher than the highest star;
You are deeper than the deepest sea;
You cherish us as your own family;
You embrace us as your own spouse;
You rule over us as your own subjects;
You welcome us as your dearest friend.
Let all the world worship you. [2]

Saint Hildegarde of Bingen
(1098–1179)

Happy, indeed, is she to whom it is given to share in this sacred banquet so that she might cling with all her heart to Him

Whose beauty all the blessed hosts of heaven unceasingly admire,

Whose affection excites,

Whose contemplation refreshes,

Whose kindness fulfills,

Whose delight replenishes,

Whose remembrance delightfully shines,

By Whose fragrance the dead are revived,

Whose glorious vision will bless all the citizens of the heavenly Jerusalem: which, since it is the splendor of eternal glory, is the brilliance of eternal light and the mirror without blemish.

Gaze upon that mirror each day, O Queen and Spouse of Jesus Christ . . .

Look at the border of this mirror, that is, the poverty of Him Who was placed in a manger and wrapped in swaddling clothes.

O marvelous humility! O astonishing poverty! The King of angels, the Lord of heaven and earth, is laid in a manger!

Then, at the surface of the mirror, consider the holy humility, the blessed poverty, the untold labors and burdens that He endured for the redemption of the whole human race. Then, in the depth of this same mirror, contemplate the ineffable charity that led Him to suffer on the wood of the Cross and to die there the most shameful kind of death.

Therefore, that Mirror, suspended on the wood of the
Cross, urged those who passed by to consider, saying:
"All you who pass by the way, look and see if there is
any suffering like my suffering!"

Let us respond with one voice, with one spirit.[3]

Saint Clare of Assisi
(*c.* 1193–1253)

My beloved Jesus Christ, I desire to enter with you into a beloved rule so that I may renew and remake my life in you. Ah! Place my life in the guardianship of your Holy Spirit so that I may keep your commandments at all times. In dear joy make my conduct suitable to you in dear peace. Flood my senses with the light of your love so that you alone may teach and guide me, and convert me within. Sink my spirit so firmly into your Spirit—quickly down into its ground—that I may be truly buried in you. And let me be so fully transported out of myself into union with you that nobody may know of my grave in you except your living love alone, which may place its seal on it. Amen.[4]

Ah, Jesus, my faithful friend, may the abyss of your generous mercy be the safest hiding-place for me, in which I may escape the horrible insults of all my enemies. And you yourself be for me then my safe asylum, into which I may joyfully leap from the captivity of all evils. Ah, Jesus, my dulcet hope, may your deific heart (broken by love for me) which lies uninterruptedly open to all sinners, be the first refuge of my soul out of its body. There, in the abyss of unlimited love, may my entire transgression be absorbed in a moment so that I may, without any obstacle, enter with you into the heavenly dance, O cherished one of my heart.[5]

Saint Gertrud of Helfta
(1256–1302)

This is the way on which the Son of God took the lead, and of which he himself gave us knowledge and understanding when he lived as Man. For from the beginning to the end of the time he spent on earth, he did and perfectly accomplished, amid multiplicity, the will of the Father in all things and at all times, with all that he was, and with all the service he could perform (Mt 20:28), in words and works, in joy and pain, in grandeur and abasement, in miracles, and in the distress of bitter death. With his whole heart and his whole soul, and with all his strength (Deut 6:5), in each and every circumstance, he was ready to perfect what was wanting on our part. And thus he uplifted us and drew us up by his divine power and his human justice to our first dignity, and to our liberty (Gal 4:31), in which we were created and loved, and to which we are now called (Gal 5:13) and chosen in his predestination (Eph 1:4–5), in which he had foreseen us from all eternity.

That cross which we must bear with the Son of the living God (Mt. 12:38) is the sweet exile that we bear for the sake of veritable Love. . . .

And thus we must always persevere with renewed ardor: with hands ever ready for all works in which virtue is practiced, our will ready for all virtues in which Love is honored, without other intention than to render Love her proper place in man, and in all creatures according to their due. This is to be crucified with Christ (Gal 2:19), to die with him, and to rise again with him (Col 3:1). To this end he must always help us; I pray him for this, calling upon his supreme goodness.[6]

Blessed Hadewijch of Brabant
(thirteenth century)

It was my King who shed those bitter tears, who bled
  Waiting in mortal dread till His betrayers led Him to be
  tormented.
Pitilessly did they strike Him and at the pillar smite Him,
Spitting in His fair face so foully to despite Him.

My King's crown is of thorns, that cruelly pierce His brow.
Alas, my joy, my love is dragged to judgment now.
Nails pierced His feet and pierced those hands so dear,
And His unblemished body was wounded with a spear.

Naked is His white breast, red is His bleeding side,
Livid His lovely face, and His wounds deep and wide:
From those five wounds, as though a crimson tide,
The blood runs down: His pains no man can hide. . . .

Bring me to Thy love: O Jesu, take my heart,
Cleanse it from every sin, and let us never part.
Thou art my whole desire: I long to be with Thee:
Kindle within me fire, that I, of earth's dross free,
May climb where I aspire, at last Thy face to see. . . .

When may I come to Thee, and in Thy melody delight,
Hearing that psalmody
That lasts eternally?
When Love His love shall bring
Then I of Love may sing.[7]

Richard Rolle of Hampole
(*c.* 1300–1349)

O eternal Truth
       what is your teaching
and what is the way
by which you want us to go to the Father,
the way by which we must go?
I know of no other road
but the one you paved
with the true and solid virtues
of your charity's fire.
You, eternal Word,
cemented with your blood,
so this must be the road.

Our sin lies in nothing else
but in loving what you hate
and hating what you love.
I confess, eternal God,
that I have constantly loved what you hate
and hated what you love.
But today I cry out in the presence of your mercy:
grant that I may follow your truth
with a simple heart;
give me the deep well and fire of charity;
give me a continual hunger
to endure pains and torments for you.
Eternal Father,
give my eyes a fountain of tears
with which to draw your mercy down
over all the world,
and especially over your bride.

Oh boundless, gentlest charity!
This is your garden,

implanted in your blood
and watered with that of your martyrs,
who ran bravely after the fragrance of your blood.
You, then, be the one to watch over it.
For who could prevail
over the city you were guarding?
Set our hearts ablaze
and plunge them into this blood
so that we may more surely conceive a hunger
for your honor
and the salvation of souls.

I have sinned against the Lord.
I have sinned!
Have mercy on me! [8]

Saint Catherine of Siena
(1347–1380)

This revelation of Christ's pains filled me full of pains, for I know well that he suffered only once, but it was his will now to show it to me and fill me with mind of it, as I had asked before. And in all this time that Christ was present to me, I felt no pain except for Christ's pains; and then it came to me that I had little known what pain it was that I had asked, and like a wretch I regretted it, thinking that if I had known what it had been, I should have been reluctant to ask for it. For it seemed to me that my pains exceeded any mortal death. I thought: Is there any pain in hell like this pain? And in my reason I was answered: Hell is a different pain, for in it there is despair. But of all the pains that lead to salvation, this is the greatest, to see the lover suffer. How could any pain be greater than to see him who is all my life, all my bliss and all my joy suffer? Here I felt unshakably that I loved Christ so much more than myself that there was no pain which could be suffered like the sorrow which I felt to see him in pain.[9]

So I was taught to choose Jesus for my heaven, whom I saw only in pain at that time. No other heaven was pleasing to me than Jesus, who will be my bliss when I am there. And this has always been a comfort to me, that I chose Jesus by his grace to be my heaven in all this time of suffering and of sorrow. And that has taught me that I should always do so, to choose only Jesus to be my heaven, in well-being and in woe.[10]

Julian of Norwich
(*c.* 1343–*c.* 1417)

If then you want to know what this desire is, truly it is Jesus, for He creates this desire in you, and He gives it to you, and it is He in you Who desires, and it is He Who desires: He is everything, and He does everything, if you could only see Him. You do nothing but allow Him to work in your soul, assenting with great joy of your heart that He vouches safe to do this in you. You, with all your reason, are nothing but an instrument with which He works; and therefore when you feel your thoughts, touched by His grace, taken up by desire towards Jesus, with a powerful and devout will to please Him and love Him, think then that you have Jesus, for it is He Whom you desire. Look at Him well, for He goes before you, not in His bodily appearance, but invisibly, through the secret presence of His power. See Him therefore in the spirit, if you can, or else believe in Him and follow Him wherever He goes, for He will lead you on the right way to Jerusalem, which is the vision of peace in contemplation.[11]

Walter Hilton
(d. 1395)

CHRIST WITH MARY AND MARTHA | *Jacopo Tintoretto (1518–1594)*

THE CATHOLIC REFORMATION

Nearly two hundred years before the Council of Trent, the need for Catholic reform was evident, and beginnings were, in fact, being made. Two Sienese saints—Catherine, the Third-Order Dominican mystic, and Bernardine, the Franciscan apostle of the Holy Name of Jesus—were precursors of the Catholic Reformation. Toward the end of the fifteenth century, it began in earnest, when Saint Catherine of Genoa established the Oratory of Divine Love, in 1490. This lay mystic is credited with setting in motion the effective reform of the Church.

When the reform movement gathered momentum, in the sixteenth century, many leaders came to the fore who were deeply and personally devoted to Christ. These included Saints Teresa of Avila and Ignatius of Loyola. The piety of this period influenced Catholic devotion right up to the twentieth century and included a profound reverence for the Blessed Sacrament. The Catholic reformers sometimes influenced subsequent generations on an intimate, personal level, as Saint Teresa did, and sometimes on an almost militant level, like Saint Ignatius.

Also included in the reform movement are representatives of the later Reformation period, which extended well into the seventeenth century. Saint Francis de Sales, for example, was deeply involved in the controversies of his time. Although he was bishop of Geneva, he never actually visited his diocese because of the conflicts between Calvinists and Catholics. Father Augustine Baker, on the other hand, was raised an Anglican, but he was equally familiar with the counterclaims of the different churches. Jean-Jacques Olier and Saint Margaret Mary belong, more properly, to the seventeenth-century French School, which carried on and in many cases brought to fruition several of the reforming ideals of the Council of Trent.

I hope that readers will find a powerful personal expression of devotion to Christ in some of these prayers.

O saving Christ, only a little while ago, you were so fearful that you lay face down in a most pitiable attitude and sweat blood as you begged your father to take away the chalice of your passion. How is it that now, by a sudden reversal, you leap up and spring forth like a giant running his race and come forward eagerly to meet those who seek to inflict that passion upon you? How is it that you freely identify yourself to those who openly admit they are seeking you but who do not know that you are the one they are seeking? Hither, hither let all hasten who are faint of heart. Here let them take firm hold of an unwavering hope when they feel themselves struck by a horror of death. For just as they share Christ's agony, His fear, grief, anxiety, sadness, and sweat (provided that they pray, and persist in prayer, and submit themselves wholeheartedly to the will of God), they will also share this consolation, undoubtedly they will feel themselves helped by such consolation as Christ felt; and they will be so refreshed by the spirit of Christ that they will feel their hearts renewed as the old face of the earth is renewed by the dew from heaven, and by means of the wood of Christ's cross let down into the water of their sorrow, the thought of death, once so bitter, will grow sweet, eagerness will take the place of grief, mental strength and courage will replace dread, and finally they will long for the death they had viewed with horror, considering life a sad thing and death a gain, desiring to be dissolved and to be with Christ.[1]

G ive me thy grace, good Lord,
to set the world at nought . . .
To bewail my sins passed;
For the purging of them patiently to suffer adversity.
Gladly to bear my purgatory here;
To be joyful of tribulations;
To walk the narrow way that leadeth to life;
To bear the cross with Christ;
To have the last thing in remembrance;
To have ever afore mine eye my death, that is ever at hand,
To make death no stranger to me;
To foresee and consider the everlasting fire of hell;
To pray for pardon before the judge come;
To have continually in mind the passion that Christ suffered
        for me;
For his benefits uncessantly to give him thanks;
To buy the time again that I before have lost.

Saint Thomas More
(1478–1535)

Written while More was a prisoner in the Tower of London

In Christ then, Who is God and Man, the True Light, the Brightness of Glory and of Eternal Light, the Spotless Mirror and Image of God; in Christ, appointed by the Eternal Father to be the Judge, Lawgiver and Savior of men; in Christ, to Whom the Holy Ghost has given testimony; and from Whom are all our merit, example, help, grace, and reward; in Whom be all our meditation and imitation; in Whom all things are sweet, learned, holy, and perfect; in Christ, Who is the light and expectation of the Gentiles, the end of the law, the salvation of God, the Father of the world to come, our final hope, Who of God is fashioned the Wisdom and Justice, Sanctification and unto us Redemption, Who with the Father and the Holy Ghost, co-eternal, consubstantial, and co-equal liveth and reigneth one God, be everlasting praise, honor, majesty, and glory, world without end. Amen.[2]

Capuchin Constitutions

(1536)

Take, Lord, and receive all my liberty, my memory, my understanding, and all my will—all that I have and possess. You, Lord, have given all that to me. I now give it back to you, O Lord. All of it is yours. Dispose of it according to your will. Give me love of yourself along with your grace, for that is enough for me.[3]

Eternal Lord of all things, I make my offering, with your favor and help. I make it in the presence of your infinite Goodness, and of your glorious Mother, and of all the holy men and women in your heavenly court. I wish and desire, and it is my deliberate decision, provided only that it is for your greater service and praise, to imitate you in bearing all injuries and affronts, and any poverty, actual as well as spiritual, if your Most Holy Majesty desires to choose and receive me into such a life and state.[4]

Saint Ignatius of Loyola
(1491–1556)

S oul of Christ, be my sanctification;
  Body of Christ, be my salvation;
Blood of Christ, fill all my veins;
Water of Christ's side, wash out my stains;
Passion of Christ, my comfort be;
O good Jesu, listen to me;
In thy wounds I fain would hide,
Ne'er to be parted from Thy side;
Guard me, should the foe assail me;
Call me when my life shall fail me;
Bid me come to Thee above,
With Thy saints to sing Thy love,
       World without end. Amen.[5]

Anima Christi

A prayer popularized (not written) by Saint Ignatius and
often included in editions of the *Spiritual Exercises*

Whoever lives in the presence of so good a friend and excellent a leader, who went ahead of us to be the first to suffer, can endure all things. The Lord helps us, strengthens us, and never fails; He is a true friend. And I see clearly, and I saw afterward, that God desires that if we are going to please Him and receive His great favors, we must do so through the most sacred humanity of Christ, in whom He takes His delight. . . .

This Lord of ours is the one through whom all blessings come to us. He will teach us these things. In beholding His life, we find that He is the best example. What more do we desire than to have such a good friend at our side, who will not abandon us in our labors and tribulations, as friends in the world do? Blessed are they who truly love Him and always keep Him at their side![6]

As often as we think of Christ we should recall the love with which He bestowed on us so many favors and what great love God showed us in giving us a pledge like this of His love, for love begets love. . . . If at some time the Lord should favor us by impressing this love on our hearts, all will become easy for us, and we shall carry out our tasks quickly and without much effort.[7]

Saint Teresa of Avila
(1515–1582)

Oh! excess of love, consecrated Host! I adore Thee within me; one heart is too little to love Thee, O my Jesus; one tongue is too little to praise Thy goodness. O my Savior, how great are my obligations to Thee, for having visited so poor a creature. I offer myself entirely to Thee in acknowledgment of so great a favor. . . .

My Jesus, give me a great devotion to Thy most holy passion, that Thy pains and Thy death may be always before my eyes, to inflame me always with love for Thee, and to incline me always to make some return of gratitude for so much love.

Give me also a great devotion to the most Holy Sacrament of the altar, in which Thou hast displayed the tenderness of Thy love for me. . . .

[F]or the sake of the Blood which Thou didst shed for me, do not permit me to betray Thee again. I pray Thee to grant me a holy death. Give me the grace to receive Thee, in my last illness, in the most holy Viaticum: that united with Thee, burning with holy flames and with an ardent desire of seeing Thee, I may depart from this world to embrace Thy feet the first time I shall behold Thee. Amen.[8]

O Jesus, the beloved of my soul, may the thought of Thy presence ever be to me as a bouquet of myrrh. Let my lips, so happy in kissing Thy sacred cross, henceforth always abstain from evil speaking, from murmurs, and all words that could displease Thee. Let my eyes, which see Thy precious blood and Thy tears flowing for my sins, regard no longer the vanities of the world, or any thing that could expose them to offend Thee. Let my ears, which listen with so much consolation to the seven words pronounced by Thee upon the cross, never take pleasure in vain praises, useless conversations, or words that could in the least wound my neighbor. Let my mind be no longer occupied with vain or evil thoughts and imaginations, after having studied with so much relish the mysteries of Thy holy cross. Let my will be ever submissive to the law of the cross, and the love of Jesus crucified, and be ever full of charity for all mankind.[9]

Saint Francis de Sales
(1567–1622)

Hail, sweet Jesus; praise, honour, and glory be to Thee, O Christ, who for my sake hast vouchsafed to come down from Thy royal seat, and from the mellifluous bosom of Thy Divine Father, into this valley of misery, and to be incarnate and made man by the Holy Ghost in the most chaste womb of the most sacred Virgin Mary. Choose, I beseech Thee, my heart for Thy dwelling-place; adorn it, replenish it with spiritual gifts, and wholly possess it.

Thou, O Lord, art called Jesus, that is to say, a Saviour: be Thou therefore my Saviour, and save me.

Give me a devout heart full of affection and compassion, whereby I may pity other men's afflictions, and may have as great feeling of their miseries as if they were my own. Grant that I may embrace all men with cheerful love and charity; may readily forgive those who offend me; may perfectly love those who hate me.[10]

Father Augustine Baker, O.S.B.
(1575–1641)

O Jesus living in Mary,
Come and live in thy servants,
In the spirit of thy sanctity,
In the fulness of thy strength,
In the reality of thy virtues,
In the perfection of thy ways,
In the communion of thy mysteries,
Be Lord over every opposing power,
In thine own Spirit, to the glory of the Father. Amen.[11]

Jean-Jacques Olier
Founder of the Sulpicians (1608–1657)

O Sacred Heart of Jesus, I give and consecrate to Thee my actions and pains, my sufferings and my life, in order that my entire being may be devoted to honor, love, and glorify Thy Sacred Heart. It is my sincere determination to be and to do all for Thy love. I renounce, with all my heart, all that may be displeasing to Thee. I choose Thee, O Sacred Heart, for the only object of my love, the protector of my life, the pledge of my salvation, the remedy of my weakness and inconstancy, the repairer of my past defects, and my safe asylum at the hour of death.

Be then, O Heart of goodness, my advocate near God the Father, and save me from His just anger. O Heart of love, in Thee I place all my confidence. I fear much from my own malice and weakness, but I hope all from Thy goodness. Destroy in me all that displeases or resists Thee. Let Thy pure love be so deeply impressed on my heart that I may never forget, or be separated from Thee. O Jesus, I implore thee, by Thy goodness to let my name be written in Thy Sacred Heart, that living and dying [as] Thy slave, I may find all my glory and happiness in Thee. Amen.[12]

Saint Margaret Mary Alacoque
(1647–1690)

First Act of Consecration to the Sacred Heart of Jesus

THE EIGHTEENTH CENTURY

The Catholic Church was attempting to recover from many attacks in the eighteenth century. It is not surprising that the prayers of that time are theological and also very devotional. The spread of printing had made reading possible for large numbers of ordinary people. There was an immense proliferation of prayer books, tracts, and other devotional works across all of Europe, Catholic and Protestant.

Along with this came a real devotional interest in the mystery of the Incarnation and in the life of Christ. Saint Louis de Montfort, who, like Saint Francis, lived a life of great poverty and preaching to the poor, is usually known as an apostle of Marian piety. He made it clear that all Christian devotion must find its ultimate source in Jesus Christ.

Saint Paul of the Cross represents a return to devotion to the Passion of Christ, which Saint Francis had popularized in the thirteenth century. There was an immense response to his preaching, and the Congregation of the Passion, which he founded, experienced considerable growth.

Saint Alphonsus Liguori, founder of the Redemptorist Order, is one of the prolific writers in Catholic history; his books were intended both for the parish priest and the ordinary Catholic faithful. They contain many meditations on the Eucharist, the Passion, and the Heart of Jesus.

On the other hand, Saint Elizabeth Bayley Seton demonstrates a piety that had its origin in Protestant or Anglican piety. She was baptized in and an active member of Trinity Church, in lower Manhattan. She became familiar with Catholicism during a visit to Italy and was particularly drawn to the Holy Eucharist. It was, in fact, devotion to the presence of Christ in the Eucharist that drew Elizabeth Seton to the Catholic Church. In Mother Seton we see certain similarities in devotion to Christ among Protestants and Catholics. It is probably a link in the ecumenical chain that has unfortunately been ignored or overlooked.

Always go to prayer with some mystery of the Sacred Passion of Jesus Christ; and, devoid of images, your understanding cleared of every other thought, enter the interior temple of your soul. By a sweet soliloquy on the mystery—in pure faith, of course—lose yourself completely in the boundless sea of divine charity. Repose there purely in God, in a sacred silence of faith and holy love, keeping the superior part of your spirit amorously attentive to the Sovereign Beloved. But do not revert to yourself; on the contrary, rest peacefully on the bosom of God.[1]

Saint Paul of the Cross
(1694–1775)

My Jesus, I long ardently
For you to come to me this day;
Without you life is misery.
Come to me soon, I pray.

Good Shepherd, bear your lost sheep home
Within your arms, whene'er I stray;
From ravening wolves that round me roam
Oh, keep me safe, I pray.

O bread of Life, for you I sigh,
Give me yourself without delay;
For otherwise my soul must die.
Give me to eat, I pray.

O fount of living waters clear,
How long and weary is the way;
Refresh my soul which thirsts for you.
Give me to drink, I pray.

Like the blind man who cried to you:
Have mercy on me, Lord, I say,
O Mary's son, that I may see;
Increase my faith, I pray.

My Lord, I knock upon your door;
Your favors I can ne'er repay,
Yet in my want I beg for more.
Fulfill my needs, I pray.

Lord, you alone are my true friend,
My treasure which can ne'er decay;
All earthly joys do you transcend.
Do visit me this day.[2]

Saint Louis de Montfort
(1673–1716)

DESPOILING OF CHRIST | *Giambattista Tiepolo (1696–1770)*

He is dead! O God! who is it that is dead? The author of life, the only-begotten Son of God, the Lord of the world,—he is dead. O death! thou wert the amazement of heaven and of all nature. O infinite love! A God to sacrifice his blood and his life! And for whom? For his ungrateful creatures; dying in an ocean of sufferings and shame, in order to pay the penalty due to their sins. Ah, infinite goodness! O infinite love!

O my Jesus! Thou art, then, dead, on account of the love which Thou hast borne me! Oh, let me never again live, even for a single moment, without loving Thee! I love Thee, my chief and only good; I love Thee, my Jesus,—dead for me! O my sorrowing Mother Mary! do thou help a servant of thine, who desires to love Jesus.[3]

O Sacrament of love, Thou who, whether Thou givest Thyself in the Communion, or dwellest on the altar, knowest, by the tender attractions of Thy love, how to draw so many hearts to Thyself, who, enamoured of Thee, and filled with amazement at the sight of such love, burn with joy, and think always of Thee; draw also my miserable heart to Thyself; for it desires to love Thee, and to live enslaved by Thy love. For my part, I now and henceforward place all my interests, all my hopes, and all my affections, my soul, my body,—I place all in the hands of Thy goodness. Accept me, O Lord, and dispose of me as Thou pleasest.[4]

A person will become perfectly holy by loving Jesus Christ, our God, our chief good, and our Savior. He himself says that anyone who loves him will be loved by the eternal Father (Jn 16:27). . . .

St. Paul, the great lover of Jesus Christ, could say "the love of Christ impels us" (2 Cor 5:14). He meant that it was not so much what Jesus Christ has suffered for us as the love he has shown in suffering for us which obliges us, and indeed forces us, to love him. Commenting on this text, St. Francis de Sales asks, "Is knowing that Jesus, true God, has loved us to the extent of suffering death on a cross for us, not like having our heart put into a wine-press, and feeling it wrenched, until love is pressed from it by a force as strong as it is loving?" . . .

The love of Jesus Christ for human beings was so great that it made him long for the hour of his death so that he might show the tenderness of his love for them. During his life, he said, "There is a baptism with which I must be baptized, and how great is my anguish until it is accomplished!" (Lk 12:50). That is why, describing the night on which Jesus began his Passion, St. John writes: "Jesus knew that his hour had come to pass from this world to the Father. He loved his own in the world and he loved them to the end" (Jn 13:1). The Redeemer called that hour "his hour" because the hour of his death was the time for which he had longed.[5]

Compassionate heart of Jesus, have mercy on me. Even before I offended you, my Redeemer, I did not deserve the great graces you have given me. You created me, gave me so many inspirations and all totally undeserved on my part. But having offended you, not only did I not deserve your favors, I certainly deserved to be abandoned by you for all eternity. But you, in your great mercy, have waited for me and preserved my life even when I was at enmity with you. Your mercy allowed me to see my misery and you called me to conversion; you gave me sorrow for my sins and a desire to love you. Now, I hope that, with your grace, I am in your friendship once again.[6]

Saint Alphonsus Liguori
(1696–1787)

O Our Lord Jesus Christ how great is the merit of that blood which abundantly redeems the whole world— and would redeem a million more—and would redeem the demons themselves if they were capable of penitence and salvation as I am—Yes Lord though your thunders should crush me and a deluge overwhelm me I will yet hope while you destroy my body you will save my soul.[7]

Saint Elizabeth Seton
(1774–1821)

THE SACRED HEART | *Anonymous, 19th century*

THE NINETEENTH CENTURY

The prayers of the nineteenth century in many ways reflect the piety of the times. This piety had two rather distinct expressions. There was the traditional Catholic piety that had come out of the eighteenth century, with many devotions and a strong theological content. It took into account that there were enemies of God and the Church in the world. The French Revolution, the collapse of Christendom in many places, and the attacks on the Church all led to an attitude of mind that was not only impious but also hostile to and condemnatory of religion. Catholic devotional life countered this attitude by imploring the divine mercy and protection and by identifying the enemies of the Church with the forces of iniquity.

I have chosen two writers who represent the traditional Catholic piety. One is Saint John Neumann, a native of Bohemia, who grew up steeped in traditional Catholic devotions, which he kept alive as bishop of Philadelphia. The city's immigrant population understood Bishop Neumann very well, and they appreciated his piety and, especially, his devotion to Christ in the Eucharist. To Neumann and his contemporaries, Christ was the Sacred Heart of Jesus, drawing people and calling them to salvation. Devotion to the Sacred Heart was the most important ingredient in cementing the different parts of the Catholic Church in the nineteenth century. Neumann and, later, Saint Thérèse give us powerful examples of this piety, which also appealed to non-Catholics, especially to simple people who had a Gospel faith. It is recorded that, at Bishop Neumann's funeral, many members of the black community were present, and most of them would not have been Catholic.

Saint Thérèse, who died at the end of the nineteenth century, brought a new dimension to traditional piety. People were not ashamed of their religious devotion, which was sometimes emotional. Saint Thérèse added a deeply loving, ardent piety, devoid of histrionics. She was a quiet, self-contained person, and it is only in her writings that we catch glimpses of the great fire of her love.

Her love for Christ was very personal. No one reading the *Story of a Soul* could question the appropriateness of her devotion, expressed in emotional terms of love.

As heirs of nineteenth-century piety, we would be wise to think about it, look into it, and be familiar with it.

The other expression of nineteenth-century Catholic devotion came from intellectual converts and is exemplified by John Henry Newman and Father Isaac Hecker, founder of the Paulists. Both were men of keen intelligence, and they were deeply involved in their religious convictions before their conversions. Newman was an Anglican priest, and Hecker was a member of the transcendentalist movement and various Christian groups. As Catholics, they expressed their devotion with the unique dimension of their own intellectual accomplishments.

Help me, dear Jesus, to grow in virtue, since I dwell so near to the fountain of living water. Help me to advance on the road to surrender, the road that leads to You, my dearly beloved Savior and my only Treasure. O my Jesus, the very thought of You fills me with a longing desire for Your love. Delay no longer to shower upon my parched soul the consolations of Your love. St. Teresa, you whose heart was so inflamed with love of Your Divine Spouse, pray for me that God may purify, justify, and sanctify me. Behold, O Jesus, my desire to love You and to give myself entirely to You.[1]

My Jesus, relieve me of my discouragement. My devotion has vanished; spiritual thoughts no longer soothe my troubled soul. Even the remembrances of Your passion and of Your Blessed Mother grow dim before my vision. O Jesus, do not forsake me. Help me, help me! I am resolved not to omit a single one of my devotions. Hear me, O my God, strengthen and increase my faith. Keep me from yielding to temptation. You said, "My yoke is sweet; my burden is light." Have mercy on me, for wheresoever I turn I see only obstacles and difficulties. Were my faith strong I would accept my trials; but alas, I feel only impatience, doubt and discouragement. My soul, hold fast to Jesus. How faint-hearted and childish I am! All my comfort, all my joy must come from You. Bring me closer to You when temptations assail me. Help me not to fail. O Lord, my God, I cast myself entirely into Your Hands. Worn out by the struggle, I will rest beneath Your cross. I embrace it. O Mother Mary, pray for me, a poor sinner; pray for me in my desolation of soul. Jesus, be merciful to me. Amen.[2]

Saint John Neumann
Bishop of Philadelphia (b. 1811, d. 1860)

I cannot penetrate Thy secret decrees, O Lord! I know Thou didst die for all men really; but since Thou hast not effectually willed the salvation of all, and since Thou mightest have done so, it is certain that Thou doest for one what Thou dost not do for another. I cannot tell what has been Thy everlasting purpose about myself, but, if I go by all the signs which Thou hast lavished upon me, I may hope that I am one of those whose names are written in Thy book. But this I know and feel most entirely, what I believe in the case of all men, but know and feel in my own case, that, if I do not attain to that crown which I see and which is within my reach, it is entirely my own fault. Thou hast surrounded me from childhood with Thy mercies; Thou hast taken as much pains with me as if I was of importance to Thee, and my loss of heaven would be Thy loss of me. Thou hast led me on by ten thousand merciful providences; Thou hast brought me near to Thee in the most intimate of ways; Thou hast brought me into Thy house and chamber; Thou hast fed me with Thyself. Dost Thou not love me? really, truly, substantially, efficaciously love me, without any limitation of the word? I know it. I have an utter conviction of it. Thou art ever waiting to do me benefits, to pour upon me blessings. Thou art ever waiting for me to ask Thee to be merciful to me.[3]

My dear Lord and Saviour, how can I make light of that which has had such consequences! Henceforth I will, through Thy grace, have deeper views of sin than before. Fools make jest of sin, but I will view things in their true light. My suffering Lord, I have made Thee suffer. Thou art most beautiful in Thy eternal nature, O my Lord; Thou art most beautiful in Thy sufferings! Thy adorable attributes are not dimmed, but increased to us as we gaze on Thy humiliation. Thou art more beautiful to us than before. But still I will never forget that it was man's sin, my sin, which made that humiliation necessary. *Amor meus crucifixus est*—"my Love is crucified," but by none other than me. I have crucified Thee, my sin has crucified Thee. O my Saviour, what a dreadful thought—but I cannot undo it; all I can do is to hate that which made Thee suffer. Shall I not do that at least? Shall I not love my Lord just so much as to hate that which is so great an enemy of His, and break off all terms with it? Shall I not put off sin altogether? By Thy great love of me, teach me and enable me to do this, O Lord. Give me a deep-rooted, intense hatred of sin.[4]

O my Lord and Saviour, in Thy arms I am safe; keep me and I have nothing to fear; give me up and I have nothing to hope for. I know not what will come upon me before I die. I know nothing about the future, but I rely upon Thee. I pray Thee to give me what is good for me; I pray Thee to take from me whatever may imperil my salvation; I pray Thee not to make me rich, I pray Thee not to make me very poor; but I leave it all to Thee, because Thou knowest and I do not. If Thou bringest pain or sorrow on me, give me grace to bear it well—keep me from fretfulness and selfishness. If Thou givest me health and strength and success in this world, keep me ever on my guard lest these great gifts carry me away from Thee. O Thou who didst die on the Cross for me, even for me, sinner as I am, give me to know Thee, to believe on Thee, to love Thee, to serve Thee; ever to aim at setting forth Thy glory; to live to and for Thee; to set a good example to all around me; give me to die just at that time and in that way which is most for Thy glory, and best for my salvation.[5]

Stay with me, and then I shall begin to shine as Thou shinest: so to shine as to be a light to others. The light, O Jesus, will be all from Thee. None of it will be mine. No merit to me. It will be Thou who shinest through me upon others. O let me thus praise Thee, in the way which Thou dost love best, by shining on all those around me. Give light to them as well as to me; light them with me, through me. Teach me to show forth Thy praise, Thy truth, Thy will. Make me preach Thee without preaching—not by words, but by my example and by the catching force, the sympathetic influence, of what I do— by my visible resemblance to Thy saints, and the evident fulness of the love which my heart bears to Thee.[6]

John Henry Newman
(1801–1890)

This week and the week past I have felt more the necessity of my giving up more and of greater self denial if I would continue to increase in the love of Jesus. Oh that I would give myself wholly up to Jesus how much more should Jesus be to me. I see in Jesus more than all the wisdom of the world and power omnipotent. . . .

In to Thy hands oh Lord I commend my spirit. Oh may I be a brave & valiant soldier in thy cause. Oh Jesus take pity on me. Thou knowest our human frailties. Forgive and bless me oh Jesus. The enemy lies always in watch of us. Jesus. Jesus. Jesus.[7]

Isaac Hecker
(1819–1888)

O Divine Word! You are the Adored Eagle whom I love and who alone attracts me! Coming into this land of exile, You willed to suffer and to die in order to draw souls to the bosom of the Eternal Fire of the Blessed Trinity. Ascending once again to the Inaccessible Light, henceforth Your abode, You remain still in this "valley of tears," hidden beneath the appearances of a white host. Eternal Eagle, You desire to nourish me with Your divine substance and yet I am but a poor little thing who would return to nothingness if Your divine glance did not give me life from one moment to the next.[8]

You know, O my God, I have never desired anything but to love You, and I am ambitious for no other glory. Your Love has gone before me, and it has grown with me, and now it is an abyss whose depths I cannot fathom. Love attracts love, and, my Jesus, my love leaps toward Yours; it would like to fill the abyss which attracts it, but alas! it is not even like a drop of dew lost in the ocean! For me to love You as You love me, I would have to borrow Your own Love, and then only would I be at rest.[9]

O Jesus, my Divine Spouse! May I never lose the second robe of my baptism! Take me before I can commit the slightest voluntary fault. May I never seek nor find anything but Yourself alone. May creatures be nothing for me and may I be nothing for them, but may You, Jesus, be everything! May the things of earth never be able to trouble my soul, and may nothing disturb my peace. Jesus, I ask You for nothing but peace, and also love, infinite love without any limits other than Yourself; love which is no longer I but You, my Jesus. Jesus, may I die a martyr for You. Give me martyrdom of heart or of body, or rather give me both. Give me the grace to fulfill my Vows in all their perfection, and make me understand what a real spouse of Yours should be. . . . [L]et me be looked upon as one to be trampled underfoot, forgotten like Your little grain of sand, Jesus. May Your will be done in me perfectly, and may I arrive at the place You have prepared for me.[10]

Saint Thérèse of Lisieux
(1873–1897)

THE HOLY FACE | *Georges Rouault (1871–1958)*

THE TWENTIETH CENTURY

Devotion to Christ in the twentieth century continued the piety of the nineteenth century but in a different environment. In the past hundred years or so, people have repeatedly questioned many details of the Gospel and called into question the difference between the Christ of faith and the historical Jesus. Some of the century's beautiful and powerful Christian writers, including Yves Congar and Romano Guardini, were critical of that approach, thinking that it took Christ away from people.

Several examples of twentieth-century Christian piety stand out. Abbot Marmion's great books present a theologically rich and well-founded piety, intellectual but never lacking in devotion. A deeply prayerful man, he sought in his own life to live the life of Christ. His writings and piety are now being rediscovered by a new generation since his recent beatification.

Alban Goodier, the missionary archbishop of Bombay, also made an immense contribution to devotion through his meditations on the life and Passion of Christ, which were standard works of Catholic piety in the 1920s and 1930s. He had a profound understanding of the theological significance of the Incarnation and how it appealed to individual human needs. In many ways, he was a precursor of the new evangelization, which calls us to speak to people where their needs are found. This is precisely what Goodier does.

Bishop Sheen's Sunday afternoon radio sermons in the 1940s were a staple in the fare of the average Catholic family in the United States. I can recall streets being deserted at 2:05

on Sunday afternoons; everyone was at home listening to Bishop Sheen. It was all the more remarkable when we remember that his sermons were never superficial. They were profound and filled with theological insights. He was devoted especially to the Passion of Christ, and for many years he preached the Good Friday "three hours" sermons in New York.

His own life reflected the immediate pre–Vatican II piety, which was a rich and informed theological blend that admirably met the needs of the people of the time. They found in Fulton Sheen's preaching a Christ who was close to them and who could help them. A great many non-Catholics also listened to Bishop Sheen and were drawn to a belief in Christianity; some found their way into the Catholic Church.

Monsignor Guardini, an Italian by birth but a German citizen, was under virtual house arrest during World War II. He strongly influenced intellectual Catholics through his work *The Lord* and his books on liturgy and the spiritual life. He took issue with those who made a distinction between the historical Jesus and the Christ of faith. He strongly believed, as I do, that such a dichotomy is unwarranted and dangerous to the faith. The short chapters of *The Lord* are well worth our meditation.

Saint Faustina, a humble Polish lay sister who had only three years of education, left a remarkable manuscript describing revelations she had of Christ as the Mercy of God. They are interesting as the work of someone with no theological background or training, and they take up several delicate theological issues without falling into obvious error. Perhaps the most daring of all her revelations is that, at the moment of death, Christ calls to every soul. She makes clear that He leaves the soul free to accept the call or not. The theological justification for such an idea can be found in the conversion of the Good Thief at the hour of death. In our time, immense numbers of people have been consoled by the Divine Mercy devotion and its beautiful image of Christ as the merciful Savior.

Terence Cardinal Cooke, archbishop of New York, was a quiet, unassuming, humble man who suffered for many years with cancer, which during the last nine years of his life was terminal. Those who knew him realized that Christ was the center of his life. He represents a generation that had been formed to a large extent by Marmion, Goodier, and Sheen. Cardinal Cooke had a simple, direct devotion to Christ as Son of God and Son of Man, who speaks to us in the face of the poor and the sick and who is waiting for us in eternal life.

The present Holy Father, Pope John Paul II, has made no secret of the fact that he is a devotional person. He has led the Rosary on television and has traveled as a pilgrim to many shrines, including those in the Holy Land. His weekly talks at Saint Peter's and his encyclicals are testaments to his devotion. Anyone who thinks that devotion in the Church is a thing of the past ought to look at the Pope's writings, which have kept devotion alive during a period when it might have been eclipsed by modernist thinking.

As we make our way through the prayers of the early martyrs and the Church Fathers, through the Dark Ages and into the medieval period, during the stormy period of the Reformation and on into modern times, we see that Pope John Paul II is an obvious heir to the Christian piety of the Church's two millennia.

L ove for His Father was the underlying motive power of every act in the life of the Incarnate Word. At the moment of completing His work, Christ declares to His Apostles that it is because He loves His Father that He is about to deliver Himself up: *Ut cognoscat mundus quia diligo Patrem* [that the world may know that I love the Father] (Jn 14:31). In that wonderful prayer which He then makes, Jesus says that He has accomplished His work which was to glorify His Father upon earth: *Ego te clarificavi super terram; opus consummavi quod dedisti mihi ut faciam* [I glorified thee on earth, having accomplished the work which thou gavest me to do] (Jn 17:4). . . .

But His love for the Father is not the only love with which Christ's Heart beats. He loves us too and in an infinite manner. It was veritably for us that He came down from Heaven, in order to redeem us and save us from death . . . For us He became incarnate, was born at Bethlehem, and lived in the obscurity of a life of toil. For us He preached and worked miracles, died and rose again. For us He ascended into heaven and sent the Holy Spirit; He still remains in the Eucharist for us, for love of us. Christ, says St. Paul, loved the Church, and delivered Himself up for her, that He might purify and sanctify her and win her to Himself (Eph 5:27).[1]

Around the Mass, the centre of all our religion, the Church organizes the worship she alone has the right to offer in the name of Christ her Spouse. . . . Throughout the year she distributes the celebration of the mysteries of her Spouse, so that each year her children may live these mysteries over again, render thanks for them to Jesus Christ and His Father, and draw from them the Divine life that these mysteries, first lived by Jesus, have merited for us.[2]

The Heart which we honor, which we adore in this Humanity united to the Person of the Word, serves here as a symbol of what? Of love. When God says to us in the Scriptures: "My son, give Me Thy heart," [Prov 23:26], we understand that the heart here signifies love. . . .

In the devotion to the Sacred Heart of Jesus we then honor the love that the Incarnate Word bears towards us. . . .

This contemplation of the benefits of Jesus towards us ought to become the source of our practical devotion to the Sacred Heart. Love alone can respond to love. . . . It is then by love, by the gift of the heart that we should respond to Christ Jesus.[3]

Blessed Columba Marmion
(1858–1923)

What is Jesus Christ to me? "Christ loved me and gave himself to me and for me"; that is what He means to me. Christ loved me, and asked me for my love; that is what He means to me. Christ loved me, and came down the lane of life looking for me, and became a child with me, and exchanged His confidences with me, and listened while I told Him my heart's desire, and told me His heart's desire in return, and gave Himself to me, and taught me how to love in a way I had never known before, nor could anyone else have taught me. Christ loved me, and let me see a little of His Heart; and I felt its trembling weakness yet leaned upon its strength; I pitied its littleness yet gloried in its greatness; I ached for its sadness yet triumphed in its glory; all within me was a turmoil of joy and anguish, and when I turned to go away I found my heart had been stolen from me. He had stolen my heart from me, and it was an agony; but an agony so sweet that I trust to have it till my dying day.[4]

What is Jesus Christ to me? He is my love in the deepest human sense of which my human heart is capable; do I need to say any more? He is my satisfaction, pressed down deep and flowing over, is not that enough? He is my inspiration: in Him, and for Him, and from Him, and with Him is my life and all that it contains: let Him take it and do with it exactly what He pleases. He is my strength and my support; when I fail He lifts me up, when I suffer He is my companion, when I am alone and despairing, He is at my side. And He is my crown; I ask for nothing more; with Him, come what may, I know I shall have enough, here in this life and for all eternity.[5]

That is the wonder of it: while He loves you, He loves me no less, while He loves you and me with all the love we creatures can receive, He loves all the world with an infinite love. Let a man learn that and it will suffice; but love Jesus Christ and you will discover all the rest. You will learn in very truth what love means; not the cramped, limping, narrowed, self-indulgent thing that men often fancy it, but the great, noble, self-sacrificing, all-embracing thing that makes a man close akin to the loving God Himself.[6]

Archbishop Alban Goodier, S.J.
(1869–1939)

Christ came to redeem us. To do this, he had to inform us who God is, and what man is in the sight of God; and this in such a way that the doors to our conversion are flung open, and we are given the strength to enter into the new. He who succeeds in this cannot be substantially judged by men. The moment man assumes the right to decide how his redeemer is or is not to be, that redeemer is reduced to human limitations, and the given conditions of human existence, as well as the whole sense of redemption, is lost. If redemption exists at all, it necessarily demands that the competence of human judgment halt before him who announces and accomplishes it. And not only relatively, with the "special consideration" due to greatness or genius, but fundamentally, because he is the Redeemer. A "savior" with human limitations is hardly worth believing in. Anyone with the least idea of what Christian life demands in the way of conversion and sacrifice knows this. If the genuine Jesus Christ were no more than the greatest of men, it would be better to hack our way alone through existence.

For Christ there is no norm; he himself is the Establisher of all norms. Once we meet him the only way he can be met, in faith; once we renounce all personal judgment, letting Scripture speak with the full weight of its authority, every line of the New Testament suddenly comes alive. The Son of God and man escapes all categories—also those of the genius or religious founder. He steps out of eternity, the unknown, an immeasurable Being revealed to us bit by bit through the word of his messengers or through some personal trait. He himself surpasses all description, though so many have attempted to tell us of him—the synoptics, Saints Paul and John and James and Jude—all speak stammeringly. And if the portraits they trace are not identical, then only because Jesus Christ can never be intellectually unified. Faith alone senses the incomprehensible oneness of his many-faceted reality with its beatific promise of eternity.

Understanding of Christ requires a complete conversion, not only of the will and the deed, but also of the mind. One must cease to judge the Lord from the worldly point of view and learn to accept his own measure of the genuine and the possible; to judge the world with his eyes. This revolution is difficult to accept and still more difficult to realize, and the more openly the world contradicts Christ's teaching, the more earnestly it defines those who accept it as fools, the more difficult that acceptance, realization. Nevertheless, to the degree that the intellect honestly attempts this right-about-face, the reality known as Jesus Christ will surrender itself. From this central reality, the doors of all other reality will swing open, and it will be lifted into the hope of the new creation.[7]

Monsignor Romano Guardini
(1885–1968)

In the terrible desert of life,
O my sweetest Jesus,
Protect souls from disaster,
For You are the Fountain of Mercy.

   Let the resplendence of Your rays,
   O sweet Commander of our souls,
   Let mercy change the world.
   And you who have received this grace, serve Jesus.

Steep is the great highway I must travel,
But I fear nothing,
For the pure fount of mercy is flowing for my sake,
And, with it, strength for the humble soul.[8]

Saint Faustina Kowalska
(1905–1938)

It is not His Sermon on the Mount that He would have remembered, but His Cross. There would have been no Gospel had there been no Cross; and the death on the Cross would have been useless for the removal of human guilt, if He had not risen from the dead. He said it behooved Him to suffer because He had to show the evil of sin, and evil is most manifest in the Crucifixion of Goodness. No greater darkness would ever descend upon the earth than that which fell upon Him on Calvary. In all other wars, there is generally a gray, or a mixture of good and evil, on both sides; but in the Crucifixion, there was black on one side and white on the other. Evil would never be stronger than it was on that particular day. For the worst thing that evil can do is not to bomb cities and to kill children and to wage wars; the worst thing that evil can do is to kill Goodness. Having been defeated in that, it could never be victorious again.

Goodness in the face of evil must suffer, for when love meets sin, it will be crucified. A God Who wears His Sacred Heart upon His sleeve, as Our Lord did when He became man, must be prepared to have human daws peck at it. But at the same time, Goodness used that very suffering as a condition of overcoming evil. Goodness took all the anger, wrath, and hate, and pleaded: "Forgive"; it took life and offered it for another. Hence to Him it was expedient that He suffer in order to enter glory. Evil, conquered in its full armor and in the moment of its monumental momentum, might in the future win some battles, but it would never win the war.[9]

Archbishop Fulton J. Sheen
(1895–1980)

Teach me, my Lord, to be sweet and gentle in all the events of life—in disappointments, in the thoughtlessness of others, in the insincerity of those I trusted, in the unfaithfulness of those on whom I relied. Let me put myself aside to think of the happiness of others, and to hide my little pains and heartaches, so that I may be the only one to suffer from them. . . .

May no one be less good for having come within my influence—no one less pure, less true, less kind, less noble for having been a fellow traveler in our journey toward eternal life. . . .

Lord Jesus, I unite myself to your perpetual, unceasing, universal sacrifice. I offer myself to you every day of my life and every moment of every day, according to your most holy and adorable will. . . . Accept my desire, take my offering, graciously hear my prayer. Let me live for love of you; let me die for love of you; let my last heartbeat be an act of perfect love. Amen.[10]

The Servant of God, Terence Cardinal Cooke
Archbishop of New York (b. 1921, d. 1983)

Try to increase your knowledge of the mystery of redemption. This knowledge will lead you to love, and love will make you share through your sacrifice in the passion of Christ. My dear children, without suffering our work would just be social work—very good and helpful, but it would not be the work of Jesus Christ, not part of the redemption. Jesus wanted to help us by sharing our life, our loneliness, our agony and death. All that He has taken upon Himself and has carried it in the darkest night. Only by being one with us has He redeemed us. We are able to do the same. All the desolation of the poor people, not only their material poverty but their spiritual destitution, must be redeemed, and we must have our share in it. Pray thus when you find it hard: I wish to live in this world which is so far from God, which has turned so much from the light of Jesus, to help them—to take upon myself something of their suffering. Yes, my dear children, let us share the sufferings of the poor, for only by being one with them can we redeem them; that is bringing God into their lives and bringing them to God.[11]

Blessed Teresa of Calcutta
(1910–1997)

In Christ and through Christ, God also becomes especially visible in his mercy; that is to say, there is emphasized that attribute of the divinity which the Old Testament, using various concepts and terms, already defined as "mercy." Christ confers on the whole of the Old Testament tradition about God's mercy a definitive meaning. Not only does he speak of it and explain it by the use of comparisons and parables, but above all *he himself makes it incarnate* and personifies it. *He himself, in a certain sense, is mercy.* To the person who sees it in him—and finds it in him—God becomes "visible" in a particular way as the Father "who is rich in mercy."[12]

Christ is the one mediator between God and mankind. . . . No one, therefore, can enter into communion with God except through Christ, by the working of the Holy Spirit. Christ's one, universal mediation, far from being an obstacle on the journey toward God, is the way established by God himself, a fact of which Christ is fully aware. Although participated forms of mediation of different kinds and degrees are not excluded, they acquire meaning and value only from Christ's own mediation, and they cannot be understood as parallel or complementary to his.

To introduce any sort of separation between the Word and Jesus Christ is contrary to the Christian faith. Saint John clearly states that the Word, who "was in the beginning with God," is the very one who "became flesh" (Jn 1:2, 14). Jesus is the Incarnate Word—a single and indivisible person. One cannot separate Jesus from the Christ or speak of a "Jesus of history" who would differ from the "Christ of faith." The Church acknowledges and confesses Jesus as "the Christ, the

Son of the living God" (Mt 16:16): Christ is none other than Jesus of Nazareth; he is the Word of God made man for the salvation of all. In Christ "the whole fullness of deity dwells bodily" (Col 2:9) and "from his fullness have we all received" (Jn 1:16). The "only Son, who is the bosom of the Father" (Jn 1:18) is "the beloved Son, in whom we have redemption.... For in him all the fullness of God was pleased to dwell, and through him to reconcile to himself all things, whether on earth or in heaven, making peace by the blood of his Cross" (Col 1:13–14, 19–20). It is precisely this uniqueness of Christ which gives him an absolute and universal significance, whereby, while belonging to history, he remains history's center and goal.[13]

Pope John Paul II
(b. 1920; elected Pope 1978)

APPENDIX

Unfortunately, there has been a tendency in modern thinking to diminish the divinity of Christ. The obvious reason for this is that modern people have trouble accepting any type of mystery, and the mystery of the Incarnation of Christ is most profound. Many Christians do not know the documents that treat of the divinity of Christ. These documents represent a straightforward interpretation of the New Testament in the early Church and in the modern Church.

Following are some excerpts from conciliar and papal pronouncements that clarify the Church's teaching on the divinity of Christ. At the time of the Protestant Reformation, none of the reformers denied these teachings. They were shared by Protestants and Catholics as well as by Orthodox Christians. It is only in recent times that there has been some undermining of belief in the divinity of Jesus of Nazareth.

We will bring this book to a close with a powerful quotation from one of the early encyclicals of Pope John Paul II, *Redemptor Hominis*, which contains many clear expressions of Christ's divinity. They reassert in modern language and thought the ancient traditions of the Church Fathers, which have their roots in the Gospels and the Pauline epistles.

The great apostle of Christ's divinity, of course, is Saint Paul. Although the evangelists make very clear that Christ is the Son of God, equal to the Father, it is Saint Paul who proclaims the doctrine of Christ's divinity to the ancient Church only twenty years or so after the crucifixion. There are numerous passages in his epistles illustrating the divinity of Christ and the saint's devotion to the Son of God. The following quotation from the epistle to the Ephesians is but one of many providing a rich meditation to strengthen our belief in Christ's divinity.

> Blessed be the God and Father of our Lord Jesus Christ, who has blessed us in Christ with every spiritual blessing in the heavenly places, even as he chose us in him before the foundation of the world, that we should be holy and blameless before him. He destined us in love to be his sons through Jesus Christ, according to the purpose of his will, to the praise of his glorious grace which he freely bestowed on us in the Beloved. In him we have redemption through his blood, the forgiveness of our trespasses, according to the riches of his grace which he lavished upon us. For he has made known to us in all wisdom and insight the mystery of his will, according to his purpose which he set forth in Christ as a plan for the fullness of time, to unite all things in him, things in heaven and things on earth.
>
> In him, according to the purpose of him who accomplishes all things according to the counsel of his will, we who first hoped in Christ have been destined and appointed to live for the praise of his glory. In him you also, who have heard the word of truth, the gospel of your salvation, and have believed in him, were sealed with the promised Holy Spirit, which is the guarantee of our inheritance until we acquire possession of it, to the praise of his glory (Eph 1:3–14).

The General Council of Chalcedon (451)[1]

Following therefore the holy Fathers, we unanimously teach to confess one and the same Son, our Lord Jesus Christ, the same perfect in divinity and perfect in humanity, the same truly God and truly man composed of rational soul and body, the same one in being (*homoousios*) with the Father as to the divinity and one in being with us as to the humanity, like unto us in all things but sin [cf. Heb 4:15]. The same was begotten from the Father before the ages as to the divinity and in the latter days for us and our salvation was born as to his humanity from Mary the Virgin Mother of God.

We confess that one and the same Lord Jesus Christ, the only-begotten Son, must be acknowledged in two natures, without confusion or change, without division or separation. The distinction between the natures was never abolished by their union but rather the character proper to each of the two natures was preserved as they came together in one person (*prosôpon*) and one hypostasis. He is not split or divided into two persons, but he is one and the same Only-begotten, God the Word, the Lord Jesus Christ, as formerly the prophets and later Jesus Christ himself have taught us about him and as has been handed down to us by the Symbol[2] of the Fathers.[3]

[1] The Council of Chalcedon declared that Jesus Christ has two natures, which are united in one divine Person.

[2] The word *Symbol* here is to be understood as a creed, or an authoritative teaching.

[3] *The Christian Faith in the Doctrinal Documents of the Catholic Church*, ed. Jacques Dupuis (New York: Alba House, 2001), 227–28.

The Second General Council of Constantinople (553)

For when we say that the only-begotten Word was united according to the hypostasis, we do not say that there took place any confusion between natures; rather, we think that God the Word was united to the flesh, each of the two natures remaining what it is. This is why Christ is one, God and man; the same, one in being (*homoousios*) with the Father as to the divinity and one in being with us as to the humanity. For the Church of God repudiates and condemns equally those who introduce a separation or division and those who introduce a confusion into the mystery of the divine incarnation.[4]

Encyclical Letter *Haurietis Aquas* (1956)

This encyclical of Pope Pius XII examines the sources in Scripture and in the mystery of the Incarnation for the devotion to the Sacred Heart of Jesus.

The Heart of the Incarnate Word is quite rightly considered the chief sign and symbol of the threefold love with which the divine Redeemer continually loves the eternal Father and all human beings. It is a symbol first of that divine love which he has in common with the Father and the Holy Spirit, but which only in him, as the Word Incarnate, is manifested to us through a weak and frail human body. [. . .] It is a symbol secondly of that burning charity which, infused into his soul, enriches the human will

[4] Ibid., 235.

of Christ; the exercise of this charity is illumined and guided by a twofold perfect knowledge, namely, beatific knowledge and infused knowledge. And finally, in a more direct and natural way, it is a symbol also of emotional affection, since the body of Jesus Christ, formed by the action of the Holy Spirit in the womb of the Virgin Mary, enjoys the most perfect powers of feeling and perception, to a greater degree in fact than the bodies of all other human beings.[5]

Pastoral Constitution *Gaudium et Spes* (1965)

In actual fact, it is only in the mystery of the Word incarnate that the human mystery becomes clear. Adam the first human being was a figure of him who was to come, namely Christ the Lord. Christ, the new Adam, fully reveals human beings to themselves in the very revelation of the Father and his love, and discloses to them their sublime calling.[. . .]

He who is the "image of the invisible God" [Col 1:15] is himself the perfect human being, who has restored to the children of Adam the divine likeness deformed by the first sin. Since in him human nature was assumed, not absorbed, it was, by that very fact, raised to a sublime dignity in us also. For by his incarnation the Son of God has united himself in some way to every person. He worked with human hands, thought with a human mind, acted with a human will, and loved with a human heart. Born of

[5] Ibid., 263–64.

the Virgin Mary, he truly became one of us, like unto us in all things except sin.

As an innocent Lamb, freely shedding his blood, he merited life for us. In him God has reconciled us with himself and among ourselves and delivered us from the bondage of the devil and of sin, so that now each one of us can say with the apostle: the Son of God "loved me and gave himself for me" [Gal 2:20]. By suffering for us, he not only set an example for us to follow in his footsteps, but he also opened up a new path. If we follow it, life and death are made holy and take on a new meaning.[6]

Encyclical Letter *Redemptor Hominis* (1979)

Jesus Christ, the Son of the living God, became our reconciliation with the Father [Rom 5:11; Col 1:20]. He it was, and he alone, who satisfied the Father's eternal love, that fatherhood that from the beginning found expression in creating the world, giving man all the riches of creation, and making him "little less than God" [Ps 8:6], in that he was created "in the image and after the likeness of God" [cf. Gen 1:26]. He and he alone also satisfied that fatherhood of God and that love which man in a way rejected by break-ing the first Covenant [cf. Gen 3:6–13] and the later covenants that God "again and again offered to man" (cf. Eucharistic Prayer IV). The Redemption of the world—this tremendous mystery of love in which creation is renewed [Gaudium et Spes, 37]—is, at its

---

[6] Ibid., 266–67.

deepest root, the fullness of justice in a human heart—the heart of the firstborn Son—in order that it may become justice in the hearts of many human beings, predestined from eternity in the First-born Son to be children of God [cf. Rom 8:29–30; Eph 1:8] and called to grace, called to love. The Cross on Calvary, through which Jesus Christ—a Man, the Son of the Virgin Mary, thought to be the son of Joseph of Nazareth—"leaves" this world, is also a fresh manifestation of the eternal fatherhood of God, who in him draws near again to humanity, to each human being, giving him the thrice holy "Spirit of truth" [cf. Jn 16:13].[7]

[7] Pope John Paul II, *Redemptor Hominis*, 9.1, in *The Encyclicals of John Paul II*, ed. J. Michael Miller, C.S.B. (Huntington, Ind.: Our Sunday Visitor, 1996), 57–58.

SOURCES

Chapter 1: The Early Martyrs

[1] Saint Polycarp, "Prayer at the Stake", in A. Hamman, O.F.M., *Early Christian Prayers*, trans. Walter Mitchell (Chicago: Henry Regnery Co.; London: Longmans, Green, 1961), 51.

[2] *Dialogue with Trypho*, 100, 5, in Hilda Graef, *Mary: A History of Doctrine and Devotion* (London: Sheed and Ward, 1963), 38.

[3] From Letter 10, in *The Liturgy of the Hours*, IV, trans. International Commission on English in the Liturgy (New York: Catholic Book Publishing Co., 1976), 1314.

[4] *Paedagogus* 3:12, in Hamman, 38–39.

[5] Fernand Cabrol, O.S.B, *Liturgical Prayer: Its History & Spirit* (reprint, Westminster, Md.: Newman Press, 1950), 118.

[6] Cabrol, 117.

Chapter 2: The Fathers of the East

[1] Melito of Sardis, "Paschal Homily", in James T. O'Connor, *The Father's Son* (Boston: St. Paul Editions), 65.

[2] Athanasius, Letter to Adelphius, in *The Teachings of the Church Fathers*, ed. John R. Willis, S.J. (San Francisco: Ignatius Press, 2002), 337.

[3] Prayer before Communion, in *My Daily Orthodox Prayer Book*, ed. Anthony M. Coniaris (Minneapolis, Minn.: Light & Life Publishing Company, 2001), 98.

[4] Ibid., 126–27.

[5] Prayer to the Suffering Christ, from "Sermon on the Passion", no. 9, in A. Hamman, O.F.M., *Early Christian Prayers*, trans. Walter Mitchell (Chicago: Henry Regnery Co.; London: Longmans, Green, 1961), 180–81.

[6] Poem 1, "Concerning his own Affairs," in *Saint Gregory of Nazianzus: Three Poems*, trans. Denis Molaise Meehan, O.S.B., vol. 75 of The Fathers of the Church (Washington, D.C.: Catholic University of America Press, 1987), 25–26.

[7] In *My Daily Orthodox Prayer Book*, 96.

[8] *Patrologia Græca* 99, 1213CD, in Christoph Schönborn, O.P., *God's Human Face: The Christ-Icon* (San Francisco: Ignatius Press, 1994), 232.

Chapter 3: The Fathers of the West

[1] From *Expositio in Psalmum 118*, Sermo xxii, quoted in Bertrand de Margerie, S.J., *An Introduction to the History of Exegesis*, vol. 2, *The Latin Fathers*, trans. Pierre de Fontnouvelle (Petersham, Mass.: Saint Bede's Publications, 1995), 112–13.

[2] From a meditation on Christ's Passion, in Vincent A. Yzermans, *Death and Resurrection: Meditations on Holy Week from the Church Fathers* (Collegeville, Minn.: The Liturgical Press, 1963), 56.

[3] From a sermon, in Yzermans, 66–68.

[4] In John Leinenweber, *Be Friends of God: Spiritual Reading from Gregory the Great* (Cambridge, Mass: Cowley Publications, 1990), 137–38.

Chapter 4: Saint Augustine

[1] From Christmas Sermon 14, in Barry Ulanov, ed., *The Prayers of St. Augustine* (Minneapolis, Minn.: The Seabury Press, 1983), 53–54.

[2] From *On the Gospel of John* 52, 2, in Ulanov, 103.

[3] From *On the Gospel of John* 2, 15, in Ulanov, 114.

[4] From *On the Christian Combat* 35, in Ulanov, 123.

[5] From Sermon cccxlix, 5, in *Leaves from St Augustine*, trans. Mary H. Allies, ed. T. W. Allies (London: Burns and Oates, 1909), 227–28.

Chapter 5: The Dark Ages

[1] From "Deer's Cry", excerpted from translation in Esther de Waal, *Every Earthly Blessing: Celebrating a Spirituality of Creation* (Ann Arbor, Mich.: Servant Publications, 1991), 15, 17.

[2] Translation of *Vexilla regis prodeunt* by Ralph Wright, O.S.B., in Benedict J. Groeschel with Kevin Perrotta, *The Journey toward God* (Ann Arbor, Mich.: Servant Publications, 2000), 81.

[3] Trans. Robin Flower, in Uinseann O Maidin, O.C.R., *The Celtic Monk: Rules and Writings of Early Irish Monks* (Kalamazoo, Mich.: Cistercian Publications, 1996), 189.

[4] Conrad Pepler, O.P., *The English Religious Heritage* (London: Blackfriars Publications, 1958), 19.

[5] *The Catholic Encyclopedia* (New York: Appleton and Company, 1907), vol. 2, 384.

[6] Ibid., 199–200.

[7] In H. A. Reinhold, ed., *The Soul Afire: Revelations of the Mystics* (Garden City, N.Y.: Image Books, Doubleday and Co., 1973), 248.

[8] In *Anglo-Saxon Poetry*, trans. R. K. Gordon (London: J. M. Dent & Sons, 1957), 235–38.

Chapter 6: The Early Middle Ages

[1] "On the Cross", in *More Latin Lyrics from Virgil to Milton*, trans. Helen Waddell, ed. Dame Felicitas Corrigan (London: Victor Gollancz Ltd, 1976), 177.

[2] "Prayer at night", ibid., 181.

[3] "In the refectory", ibid., 185.

[4] In *Ancestral Prayers*, compiled by F. A. Gasquet (Springfield, Ill.: Templegate Publishers, 1996), 38–39.

[5] Ibid., 11–13.

[6] In *The HarperCollins Book of Prayers*, compiled by Robert Van de Weyer (HarperSanFrancisco, 1993), 158–59.

[7] *The Roman Missal: The Sacramentary*, trans. International Commission on English in the Liturgy (New York: Catholic Book Publishing Co., 1974), 1006–7.

Chapter 7: The Monks

[1] From Sermon 15, *On the Song of Songs*, trans. Kilian Walsh, O.C.S.O. (Spencer, Mass.: Cistercian Publications, 1971), 110.

[2] "Sermon on the Lord's Nativity", in Ewert Cousins, "The Humanity and the Passion of Christ", *Christian Spirituality: High Middle Ages and Reformation*, ed. Jill Raitt (New York: Crossroad, 1988), 380.

[3] "Prayer to Christ", in Cousins, 377–78.

[4] From Meditation I of Saint Anselm, in William H. Shannon, *Anselm: the Joy of Faith* (New York: Crossroad, 1999), 73–74.

[5] Meditation 10 from *The Works of William of St.-Thierry*, vol. 1, *On Contemplating God, Prayer, Meditations*, trans. Sr. Penelope, C.S.M.V. (Spencer, Mass.: Cistercian Publications, 1971), 153, 154.

[6] Aelred of Rievaulx, *The Mirror of Love*, chap. 5, in Eric Colledge, *The Mediæval Mystics of England* (New York: Charles Scribner's Sons, 1961), 109–10.

Chapter 8: The Friars

[1] *Francis of Assisi: Early Documents*, ed. Regis J. Armstrong, O.F.M. Cap., et al. (New York: New City Press, 1999), vol. 1, 81–83.

[2] Armstrong, 156.

[3] From the *Life of Saint Francis* by Thomas of Celano, in *The Prayers of Saint Francis*, compiled by W. Bader (Hyde Park, N.Y.: New City Press, 1996), 29.

[4] From *Little Flowers of St. Francis*, ibid., 31. This prayer was composed when the saint was being tormented by evil spirits.

[5] From *Mirror of Perfection*, ibid., 38.

[6] *Saint Anthony: Herald of the Good News*, trans. Claude M. Jarmak, O.F.M. Conv. (Ellicott City, Md.: Conventual Franciscan Friars, 1995), 37.

[7] Ibid., 71.

[8] Ibid., 145.

[9] Ibid., 176–77.

Chapter 9: The Medieval Theologians

[1] Translated from the text in P. G. Meersseman, O.P., *Introductio in Opera Omnia B. Alberti Magni OP* (Bruges: Charles Beyaert, 1931), 123.

[2] Saint Bonaventure, *De triplici via*, II, chap. 3, § 5, in Dom Jean Leclercq et al., *The Spirituality of the Middle Ages*, vol. 2 of *A History of Christian Spirituality* (New York: The Seabury Press, 1982), 310.

[3] "Verbum Supernum Prodiens" (part of Saint Thomas' Office for Corpus Christi), in *Devoutly I Adore Thee: The Prayers and Hymns of St. Thomas Aquinas*, trans. and ed. Robert Anderson and Johann Moser (Manchester, N.H.: Sophia Institute Press, 1993), 97–99.

[4] "Adoro te devote", in *More Latin Lyrics from Virgil to Milton*, trans. Helen Waddell, ed. Dame Felicitas Corrigan (London: Victor Gollancz Ltd., 1976), 307, 309.

Chapter 10: The Mystics

[1] "Ode for the Wednesday of Holy Week", quoted in H. J. W. Tillyard, *Byzantine Music and Hymnography* (London: The Faith Press, 1923), 30.

[2] In the *HarperCollins Book of Prayers*, compiled by Robert Van de Weyer (HarperSanFrancisco, 1993), 196.

[3] From the fourth letter to Blessed Agnes of Prague, in *Francis and Clare: The Complete Works*, ed. and trans. Regis J. Armstrong, O.F.M. Cap., and Ignatius C. Brady, O.F.M. (The Classics of Western Spirituality; New York: Paulist Press, 1982), 204–5.

[4] *Gertrud the Great of Helfta: Spiritual Exercises*, trans. Gertrud Jaron Lewis and Jack Lewis (Kalamazoo, Mich.: Cistercian Publications, 1989), 65–66.

[5] Ibid., 116.

[6] Letter 6 in *Hadewijch: The Complete Works*, trans. Mother Columba Hart, O.S.B. (New York: Paulist Press, 1980), 62–63.

[7] "A Meditation on Christ's Passion", in *The Mediæval Mystics of England*, ed. Eric Colledge (New York: Charles Scribner's Sons, 1961), 150–51.

[8] In *The Prayers of Catherine of Siena*, ed. and trans. Suzanne Noffke (San Jose/New York: Authors Choice Press, 2001), 70–71.

[9] *Julian of Norwich: Showings*, trans. and ed. Edmund Colledge, O.S.A., and James Walsh, S.J. (New York: Paulist Press, 1978), 209.

[10] Ibid., 212–13.

[11] Walter Hilton, *The Scale of Perfection*, chap. 24, in *The Mediæval Mystics of England*, 256–57.

Chapter 11: The Catholic Reformation

[1] *The Sadness of Christ, and Final Prayers and Instructions*, ed. Gerard Wegemer, trans. Clarence Miller (Princeton, N.J.: Scepter Publishers, 1993), 75, taken from *Complete Works of Thomas More*, vol. 14: *De Tristitia Christi* (Yale University Press, 1976).

[2] The Capuchin Constitutions of 1536, chap. 12, no. 152, quoted in John C. Olin, *The Catholic Reformation: Savonarola to Ignatius Loyola* (New York: Fordham University Press, 1992), 181.

[3] *The Spiritual Exercises of Saint Ignatius*, trans. George E. Ganss, S.J. (Chicago: Loyola University Press, 1992), 95.

[4] Ibid., 55.

[5] Translated by Cardinal John Henry Newman; see *Prayers, Verses, and Devotions* (San Francisco: Ignatius Press, 1989), 314.

[6] *The Book of Her Life*, chap. 22, in *The Collected Works of St. Teresa of Avila*, vol. 1, trans. Kieran Kavanaugh, O.C.D., and Otilio Rodriguez, O.C.D. (Washington, D.C.: ICS Publications, 1976), 194.

[7] Ibid., 198.

[8] "Aspirations of Love", from *Visitation Manual* (New York: George Grady Press, 1955), 225–26.

[9] "Prayer to Jesus Crucified," in ibid., 284–85.

[10] Augustine Baker, *Sancta Sophia* [*Holy Wisdom*], ed. Dom Norbert Sweeney, O.S.B. (London: Burns and Oates, 1876), 567, 568, 570, 571.

[11] Quoted in John Saward's "Bérulle and the 'French School'", in *The Study of Spirituality*, ed. Cheslyn Jones, Geoffrey Wainwright, and Edward Yarnold, S.J. (London: SPCK, 1986), 396.

[12] From *Visitation Manual.*

Chapter 12: The Eighteenth Century

[1] In Father Brice, C.P., *In Spirit and in Truth: The Spiritual Doctrine of Saint Paul of the Cross* (New York: Frederick Pustet Co., 1948), 253.

[2] Saint Louis Marie de Montfort, "Mille fois mon coeur vous désire", in *God Alone: The Collected Writings of St. Louis Marie de Montfort* (Bay Shore, N.Y.: Montfort Publications, 1997), 539–40.

[3] Meditation XIII for Holy Thursday, in *The Complete Works of Saint Alphonsus de Liguori*, ed. Eugene Grimm, C.Ss.R., vol. 5, *The Passion and the Death of Jesus Christ* (Brooklyn, N.Y.: Redemptorist Fathers, 1927), 454.

[4] *The Holy Eucharist*, in *The Complete Works of Saint Alphonsus* (ed. Grimm), vol. 6, 149–50.

[5] Saint Alphonsus Liguori, *The Practice of the Love of Jesus Christ*, chap. 1, trans. Brendan McConvery, C.Ss.R., in *Alphonsus de Liguori: Selected Writings*, ed. Frederick M. Jones, C.Ss.R. (The Classics of Western Spirituality; New York: Paulist Press, 1999), 112–15.

[6] Ibid., 232.

[7] In Annabelle M. Melville, *Elizabeth Bayley Seton* (New York: Charles Scribner's Sons, 1951), 289.

Chapter 13: The Nineteenth Century

[1] Prayer for Holiness, in *Saint John Neumann's Favorite Prayers Taken from His Diary* (Philadelphia: Saint John Neumann Shrine, n.d.), 24–25.

[2] Prayer in Discouragement, in ibid., 36–38.

[3] John Henry Newman, meditation, "Our Advocate Above", repr. in *Prayers, Verses, and Devotions* (San Francisco: Ignatius Press, 2000), 412–13.

[4] From "The Heinousness of Sin", repr. in ibid., 371–72.

[5] From "Jesus Our Guide and Guardian", repr. in ibid., 277.

[6] From "Jesus the Light of the Soul", repr. in ibid., 389–90.

[7] From a diary entry of January 22, 1845, in *Isaac T. Hecker: The Diary*, ed. John Farina (New York: Paulist Press, 1988), 302–3.

[8] From *Story of a Soul: The Autobiography of Saint Thérèse of Lisieux*, trans. John Clarke, O.C.D. (Washington, D.C.: ICS Publications, 1996), 199.

[9] Ibid., 256.

[10] From a letter written on the day Saint Thérèse made her profession, September 8, 1890, in ibid., 275.

Chapter 14: The Twentieth Century

[1] Abbot Columba Marmion, O.S.B., *Christ in His Mysteries*, trans. Mother M. St. Thomas (St. Louis, Mo.: B. Herder, 1939), 11.

[2] Columba Marmion, O.S.B., *Christ, the Life of the Soul* (St. Louis, Mo.: B. Herder, 1922), 96.

[3] *Christ in His Mysteries*, 369, 373.

[4] Alban Goodier, S.J., *Jesus Christ the Son of God* (London: Burns Oates & Washbourne, 1920), 139–40.

[5] Ibid., 142.

[6] Ibid., 143.

[7] Romano Guardini, *The Lord*, trans. Elinor Castendyk Briefs (Chicago: Regnery Gateway, 1982), 534–35.

[8] Saint Maria Faustina Kowalska, *Diary: Divine Mercy in My Soul* (Stockbridge, Mass.: Marians of the Immaculate Conception, 2000), 383.

[9] Fulton J. Sheen, *Life of Christ* (New York: McGraw-Hill, 1958), 522.

[10] Terence Cardinal Cooke, *Prayers for Today* (New York: Alba House, 1991), 82–83.

[11] Mother Teresa to her Sisters of the Missionaries of Charity, July 16, 1993, in J. Neuner, S.J., "Mother Teresa's Charism," in *Vidyajyoti: Journal of Theological Reflection* (March 2001), 181.

[12] *Dives in Misericordia*, 2.2, repr. in *The Encyclicals of John Paul II*, ed. J. Michael Miller, C.S.B. (Huntington, Ind.: Our Sunday Visitor, 1996), 112.

[13] *Redemptoris Missio*, 5.4, 6.1, in ibid, 498–99.

ART CREDITS

PAGE 72

Vision of Saint Thomas Aquinas

Sassetta (Stefano di Giovanni) (c. 1400–1450)

Pinacoteca, Vatican Museums, Vatican State

© Scala / Art Resource, New York

PAGE 80

"Scivias" (Know the ways of the Lord) by Saint Hildegarde von Bingen
    (1098–1179)

The book, *Codex Rupertsberg*, disappeared during WW II

Image is from a facsimile: Fear of God (the blue sphere) and God
enthroned upon man's faith

Romanesque, 12th century

© Erich Lessing / Art Resource, New York

PAGE 92

Christ with Mary and Martha

Jacopo Robusti Tintoretto (1518–1594)

Alte Pinakothek, Munich, Germany

© Scala / Art Resource, New York

PAGE 108

Despoiling of Christ

Giambattista Tiepolo (1696–1770)

S. Polo, Venice, Italy

© Scala / Art Resource, New York

PAGE 112

The Sacred Heart

Anonymous, 19th century

Color engraving, 34 x 23 cm

Private Collection, France

© Giraudon / Art Resource, New York

PAGE 122

The Holy Face

Georges Rouault (1871–1958), © ARS, New York

© Art Resource, New York

ACKNOWLEDGMENTS

The Catholic University of America Press, Washington, D.C.

For permission to reprint excerpts from "Concerning his own Affairs" in *Saint Gregory of Nazianzus: Three Poems*, translated by Denis Molaise Meehan, O.S.B.

Congregation of Marians of the Immaculate Conception, Stockbridge, Mass., 01263

For permission to reprint excerpts from *Diary of Divine Mercy in My Soul*, by St. Maria Faustina Kowalska. Copyright © 1987.

The Continuum Publishing Group

For permission to reprint excerpt from *Dialogue with Trypho*, quoted in Hilda Graef, *Mary: A History of Doctrine and Devotion*. Copyright © 1963 by Sheed and Ward.

For permission to reprint excerpts from Sermon cccxlix of St. Augustine, quoted in *Leaves from St. Augustine*, published by Burns and Oates.

For permission to reprint excerpts from *Sancta Sophia*, by Fr. Augustine Baker, O.S.B., edited by Dom Norbert Sweeney, O.S.B., published by Burns and Oates.

For permission to reprint excerpts from the *Meditations and Devotions* of John Henry Newman, published by Burns and Oates, Ltd.

For permission to reprint excerpts from *Jesus Christ the Son of God*, by Most Rev. Alban Goodier, S.J., published by Burns Oates & Washbourne, Ltd.

Conventional Franciscan Friars, St. Anthony of Padua Province, U.S.A.

For permission to reprint excerpts from *Saint Anthony: Herald of the Good News*, translated by Claude Jarmak, O.F.M. Conv. Copyright © 1995.

HarperCollins Publishers, Inc.

For permission to reprint excerpts from *The Prayers of St. Augustine*, by Barry Ulanov. Copyright © 1983 by Barry Ulanov.

others, from The Classics of Western Spirituality. Copyright © 1999 by the Dublin Province of the Congregation of the Most Holy Redeemer, Paulist Press, Inc.

For permission to reprint excerpts from *Isaac T. Hecker: The Diary: Romantic Religion in Ante-Bellum America*, edited by John Farina. Copyright © 1988 by John Farina, from The Sources of American Spirituality, Paulist Press, Inc.

Regnery Publishing, Inc., Washington, D.C.

For permission to reprint excerpts from *The Lord*, by Romano Guardini, translated by Elinor C. Briefs. Copyright © 1982. Published by Regnery Publishing, Inc. All rights reserved.

Simon & Schuster Adult Publishing Group

For permission to reprint excerpts from Aelred of Rievaulx, Richard Rolle, and Walter Hilton, from *The Mediæval Mystics of England*, translated and edited by Eric Colledge. Copyright © 1961 by Charles Scribner's Sons.

For permission to reprint excerpts from *Elizabeth Bayley Seton 1774– 1821*, by Annabelle Melville. Copyright © 1951, 1960, 1976 by Annabelle Melville.

Templegate Publishers (www.templegate.com)

For permission to reprint excerpts from *Ancestral Prayers*, compiled by F. A. Gasquet. Copyright © 1996 by Templegate Publishers.